Preaching Sex

on love, intimacy, power, abuse

Gary Harder

with
Lydia Neufeld Harder

To our parents,
Margarete and Cornelius Neufeld,
and George and Susie Harder,
who lived out marriage and family life
with such love, intimacy, and respect.

Contents

Part Four
Weddings and Marriage

Part Five
Appendix: Resources

Foreword by Carol Penner

"Who wants to read a collection of old sermons?" was my first reaction when I heard about this book. Sermons are time- and location-sensitive, as they are delivered to a specific audience at a particular moment in time. I wasn't sure a retrospective book of sermons would be relevant for today's readers, but I was delighted to find a book that is fascinating, instructive and still resonates with issues we face today.

The sermons span a time period when immense social changes were happening in North America around gender, power and relationships. As the book unfolded, I was continually amazed at Gary and Lydia's courage to preach on risky and controversial subjects. Some of the sermons are so incisive, it would be challenging to preach them even today.

It's significant that many of the sermons were developed with a preaching team. Gary outlines how this worked; four laypeople were selected by the congregation to assist in choosing the texts and developing the theme with the preacher. The sermons reflect not only the thoughts of one person but also a direction set by a leadership team. A congregation would have heard some of these controversial sermons knowing that it was the wisdom of the group bringing a topic to the fore.

Congregations have a greater capacity for hearing edgy sermons if they truly know their pastor loves them. They simply trust that their pastor has their best interests at heart. These sermons are a testimony to the strong pastoral bonds that Gary and Lydia forged with their congregations through long pastorates.

At several points, Gary speaks of his own identity as a heterosexual man, and how that shaped his view of these issues. In a Christian tradition deeply shaped by patriarchal forces, that identity also gave him authority, and he used that power to address inequalities.

Some of the sermons made me gasp at their straightforward denunciation of patriarchy. I was preaching at a similar time, and I rarely spoke so candidly to my congregations. I think it was more difficult for women and other groups to address power imbalances. However, many male pastors never used their power to do the important work that is evidenced here.

I can only imagine how significant it was for people who were caught in abusive relationships, exploring their gender, or untangling sexist practices to hear their pastors preaching on these topics.

The contexts for most of the sermons were urban churches, where many in the congregations were well-educated or worked in professional settings. However, Gary himself came out of a rural church environment. It is so refreshing to read sermons that exude a mix of both confidence and humbleness, when a preacher can say, "I'm still not sure I know what I'm talking about."

The cover of the book advertises the "boldly biblical" nature of their writing, and it truly lives up to this description. Both Gary and Lydia treat the biblical text with respect, believing that God has good news for us, even in the most difficult passages. Readers will find good news here: I was delighted and intrigued and challenged by these sermons. For a book that talks about brokenness, there was a lot of joy bubbling up as well.

I think the book is immensely useful to preachers and pastors in training who have the power to choose texts and explore themes that are liberative. Gary and Lydia show how careful biblical engagement, humour, honest reflection on personal experience and observations about culture can be woven together.

Preachers can ask themselves, "At the end of my career, how will I have preached on these topics; how will I have shepherded my flock through these thorny issues?" I think this book gives courage and resolve to pastors, who need encouragement to speak on vital issues that affect us all.

I have immense respect for Gary and Lydia as pastors and thinkers. I certainly look to them both as faithful people who think deeply about love, intimacy, power and abuse; they are some of the wisest people I know. I am so thankful for Gary and Lydia's rich and fruitful service to God and for their decision to share these resources with the wider church. They remind us of the faithfulness of God in the midst of both our love stories and our brokenness.

Dr. Carol Penner,
Director of Theological Studies,
Conrad Grebel University College
University of Waterloo, Canada

Preface

Last spring, we were downsizing in preparation for our relocation from Toronto to Waterloo. Getting rid of way too much furniture was relatively easy. Family, for the most part, was eager to take most of it. But there was that long shelf of old binders filled with old sermons. So, what to do with 55 years' worth of sermons collecting dust? At least look at them.

As I was glancing over the sermons, throwing away most of them, we in Mennonite Church Eastern Canada (MCEC) were again confronted in our Mennonite media by stories of sexual abuse by pastors. My heart ached for the survivors. I wondered how I, as pastor, had addressed this issue in my preaching and writing. I read my sermons through a new lens. I noticed that I had actually preached and written articles about sexuality quite often. The Bible carries many stories of even heroes of faith who are sexually abusive. There are also visions of healthy intimacy and sexuality.

I collected the sermons I had preached and the articles I had written around the general themes of sexuality, abuse, and intimacy. Could they make a book? I still don't know. But I was inclined to sort them out, bring them together, and put them into a form accessible for anyone interested – probably only my family. But as I worked with my wife, Lydia, and the book took shape with the publisher, I became aware that a half-century of social change is reflected in this collection. My hope for this book is that it might energize discussions, debates, and learnings around sexuality.

We live in an "overly sexualized world." And yet, it seems difficult to talk freely about sex in the church. What makes for healthy sexuality and deeply intimate relationships? How do we open conversations about sex in our homes and the church? I never knew how to start these conversations in my own home with my children. I found it easier to do this in the churches where I was pastor or with couples wanting to get married. Why wasn't I comfortable having these discussions with my own children? I didn't see myself as a radical – definitely not militantly progressive in my views. More like 'boldly biblical.' I was fairly modest or moderate but not meek.

And what about sexual abuse? How do we challenge it, especially in the church? That's hardly a task for the meek. Or modest. What roadmaps do we have to bring to light to engage and confront unhealthy and abusive sexuality? And – equally important – how do we foster education, discussion, and teaching around healthy sexuality – the good gift of our Creator?

The Bible has always been a source of inspiration, challenge, puzzlement, delight, despair, and awe over how it deals with the reality of our sexual lives. Its stories call out for preaching. But these stories offer no consistent guide for such preaching, nor, for that matter, a consistent theology of sexuality. Throughout my half-century of preaching, I've returned to texts time and again to encounter new – bolder – insights while also approaching them with humility and curiosity. We are left trying to sort out important things with wonderful stories but no clear road map.

All good preaching grows out of context – both our contemporary context and the context referred to in the biblical texts. That is the challenge and opportunity – and danger – of preaching about human sexuality. The context of my ministry gave me the chance to officiate at weddings and celebrate the loving commitment that these ceremonies represented. That is a context where a pastor has the privilege to preach positively about sex. Don't we all need those sorts of healthy discussions in church?

I delighted in doing marriage preparation with so many couples. But I also walked with so many people who were wounded by sexual abuse. Their stories carried so much pain. I couldn't keep silent. I knew I needed to preach about sex – about healthy sexuality and about abusive sexuality.

But if preaching at its best is contextual, "old" sermons are soon dated, aren't they? There are always new challenges, new perspectives, and new issues to respond to, aren't there? Yes. And no. We continue to hear stories of sexual abuse – including by church leaders. There is so much pain around damaging sexual relationships. But we also have the opportunity to envision healthy sexuality and healthier sexual relationships.

And what about us preachers? We too – young or old, male or female, heterosexual, bisexual, gay, or queer – are also sexual beings navigating our sexuality, with both its complex beauty and its challenges. We haven't got it all figured out in our personal lives either. We need to be humble and accountable and admit when we struggle.

I am reminded of Ecclesiastes 9:20: "Surely there is no one on earth so righteous as to do good without ever sinning." In his response to the Pharisees, who brought a woman caught in adultery to him, Jesus said that anyone who is without sin should cast the first stone, and no one there could (John 8:3-11). We too acknowledge our humanness, the challenges in our relationships, and the complexities of our sexual lives. We all need to be touched by God's love, forgiveness, and healing.

All sermons are, of course, both dated and contextual. As I re-read sermons from the first years of my ministry, I shudder at the "male" language I consistently used. But then, even my "feminist theologian" wife didn't take me to task for it at that time. I have decided to leave these sermons mostly intact, with only minor editing. Times change, and the same unchanging Bible looks different to us at times.

Many of us were ignorant of, or ignored, the complexities around gender identity and sexual orientation twenty or thirty years ago. I confess that the earlier sermons do not deal with questions around LGBTQ+ directly, though intimacy and abuse are relevant for all of us, no matter how we name ourselves. I also acknowledge that the reader might notice a few "repetitions," notably of the creation stories from Genesis because I see them as touchstones of our theology of sexuality. These sermons interpret the Genesis account for a context in which patriarchy ruled. However, the interpretations can also lead us to think in a binary way, as if there are only two sexual natures. I acknowledge that more work needs to be done to find ways to speak inclusively of all people.

I am so grateful that the two churches where I served as pastor for longer periods – First Mennonite Church Edmonton and Toronto United Mennonite Church (TUMC) – were so open to my fumbling attempts to explore and preach about healthy and abusive sexuality.

I am especially grateful to my wife Lydia, my companion, my confidant, my critic, my partner in intentional ministry after my retirement from full-time ministry, my supporter, and my lover. We have delighted in our partnership and have felt free to challenge each other over, well,— over many things, both theological and practical.

Waterloo, Ontario

October 2023

Introduction: An Interview with the Author

Q1. *Why did you decide to collect these sermons, and who was your intended readership?* I initially collected these sermons for my children and grandchildren but realized they might also be helpful discussion starters for people in the church. I want to encourage pastors and churches to be free to talk about sex – its beauty and power – but also how that power can be – and has been – abused, especially by leaders in the church. Yes, I do want my grandchildren to know that their "old" grandpa has freely preached about sex quite a lot. I hope it brings a smile to their faces and maybe even an opportunity for conversation.

Q2. *Were you raised to think of sexuality as positive or positively sinful?* My parents never did talk to me about sex, not even to warn me in any way to be "pure." However, I knew that my parents had a very healthy marriage relationship and a deep respect for each other. They modeled a very good marriage relationship. They were not open or public about their sexual attraction for each other – though I did hear their creaking bed a few times and knew what was going on. I think that somehow pleased me to know they loved each other that way. I did assume – I don't know if I was taught this – that full sexual expression belonged within marriage. We farm children saw a lot of sexual activity in our farm animals. That was a normal part of life.

It wasn't until my final high school year (at Rosthern Junior College) that I heard a guest preacher warn us about the evils of masturbation. I also became aware of hesitancy about dancing and the temptations associated with it and understood that premarital sex was frowned upon. I heard of some couples who had to confess before the church their sin of having sex before marriage, as evidenced by pregnancy. At Canadian Mennonite Bible College (CMBC), David Schroeder helped us learn that it was good to talk about sex. In fact, couples needed to talk to each other about sex early enough that they understood each other and knew each other's boundaries.

Q3. *Is there still a place for encouraging modesty?* I do respect our "Mennonite modesty" tradition, especially when modesty means honestly presenting ourselves without emphasizing only our physical sexuality. But there is also something positive about dressing to be attractive and to feel good about oneself. Yet if this leads to flaunting our sexuality, this may hide what is more basic to who we are. Yet I am also not comfortable with the idea that modesty is only for women. Men can also use their bodies and the way they dress to show off and provoke sexual desire without a willingness to enter into a committed relationship. Immodest clothing can potentially be a part of the grooming for abuse.

Q4. *If a pastor is providing pre-marital counseling, should they talk about sexuality? How?* I assume that pastors need to talk about sexuality in pre-marriage counseling. I am not content with simply giving out a book, no matter how good the book is. There is a huge opportunity here to process the fullness of what an intimate relationship can contain — including wholesome sexuality. I used a "flower of intimacy" model to discuss the fuller meaning of relationship and intimacy (see Appendix). It identified ten petals, one of which was physical intimacy, meaning sex. Many couples have been living together before marriage. Rather than condemning that, I liked to explore with the couple their experience of those facets of intimacy, and then think of ways to enrich each of them.

Q5. *What surprised or shocked you most as you read the Bible on the topic of sexuality?* The surprise, in many ways, was how often, straightforwardly and matter-of-factly, the Bible talks about human sexuality. It deals with the reality of human life, both the painful and abusive, but also the beauty and joy of human sexuality. This is especially true in the stories. The moral teachings are only a small part of what the Bible says. I remember being horrified when I read the stories about our heroes of faith and the rape, violence, and power abuse that they committed, e.g., the story of Tamar.

Q6. *Song of Songs used to be the favourite book for writing commentaries in the medieval era. Now, it seems taboo.* I love that the Song of Songs is in the Bible, and think it should definitely be kept in the canon of Scripture. Pastors should preach from it, and youth should be encouraged to read it. It is a very poetic and beautiful picture of a healthy, mature sexual relationship. It can lead to great discussions if a teacher or pastor can get over their own embarrassment (or modesty).

Q7. *A few passages in Scripture deal with celibacy and abstinence (Matt 19, 1 Cor 7), but you haven't addressed these here. Should celibacy be encouraged at all?* I am a bit surprised that I haven't included these two texts. I have not deliberately neglected them; they are certainly worth preaching about. Christina Reimer has focused in her scholarship on how these verses have been used. There may be various reasons to be celibate, perhaps even some painful ones, but that is a choice that deserves respect. However, virginity pledges and movements that promote chastity and purity for young people, I think, can be very unhealthy. To me, they sound like they are directed by men and arise out of a patriarchal view of the husband/father assuming the role of protector of women. Instead, girls and women need to claim power over their own bodies and sexual nature. Everyone needs to be taught about the signs of abuse and how to understand and respect consent.

Q8. Power abuse by church leaders has been said to be the most devastating issue for the church's credibility today. How can "preaching sex" support the rebuilding of clarity and trust? My hope is that this book may create a safer atmosphere to talk about all aspects of our sexual lives, including the incredibly painful experiences some people had when they were abused by church leaders. In our circles, we now insist on "safe church policies," boundary awareness, accountability structures of leaders, support for survivors, and a readiness to support "victim-whistleblowers." Let's talk more freely about all aspects of our sexual lives in church so that we surround ourselves with the good news of healthy sexuality. It is debilitating and disempowering when the only thing we hear about sex in the church is when it has been abused.

Q9. In what ways has your reflection on the Mennonite faith tradition and the changing culture in Canadian society impacted your views on sexuality? There certainly are aspects of our consumer culture that need to be challenged. Much of consumer culture around sexuality seems to see sex as a "commodity" rather than as an important aspect of deep relationships. Our Mennonite faith tradition has talked about wholeness of life under God and the caring community aspect of living out our faith. We will obviously be impacted by the changing culture in Canada (including shifting sexual mores), but we have significant lenses in our heritage that we can examine and test what is healthy and what is unhealthy as the world keeps changing. God created us humans as sexual beings and named this gift "good." God built "mutuality" and "relationship" into our very beings.

Q10. *One of your early professors at seminary was John H. Yoder, who was highly influential for many people of your generation but was later found to have sexually abused a large number of women throughout his career. How did that news change your view of his teaching, particularly on nonviolent ethics?* This is a particularly challenging question to answer. Shortly before reports of Yoder's sexual abuse came out, I worked with him during an ecumenical week-long peace conference held at Newman College, a Catholic institute in Edmonton. Because he was a Mennonite, the council chose me, also a Mennonite, to be chaplain for the week's events. We even had John in our home and it wasn't long after this that word started coming out about his sexual abuse. Lydia and I felt devastated – and confused. How could that be, given his teaching and writing about peace? I had absorbed his theology in seminary. I don't have the tools anymore to "demythologize" his theology, but it seems to me that his central teaching of "revolutionary subordination" and obedience sounded to females like he is requiring submission – it made them afraid to speak out and to challenge his abuse. For men, it gave them the illusion that they could give up their power by claiming to be powerless – a recipe for abuse to happen and to be justified theologically.

Lydia worked at challenging Yoder theologically and her doctoral thesis was on obedience and suspicion.[1] Mennonite feminism challenged Yoder most directly, precisely because his theology could be used to justify abuse and disempower women.

Q11. *Is there a unique Mennonite contribution to the question of healthy sexuality today?* Yes, I think there is. We have a theology that highlights peace in all aspects of life, including our personal relationships – especially in our intimate relationships. It also highlights community. We don't keep everything private. When something is right, we celebrate it together. When something is wrong (like abuse), we name it as a community and support each other in dealing with it. And, more recently, as we have embraced and celebrated the leadership of women in the church, we have far more resources and far more leaders to help us navigate the treacherous waters of abuse and envision a much healthier sexuality. We are becoming more aware of power issues within personal relationships, not only in geopolitics. We need to go beyond non-resistance (the recently published book *Resistance*, edited by Carol Penner and Cameron Altaras, 2022, is an excellent resource here).

Q12. *How does a theology of nonviolence and reconciliation best apply when there is abuse or sexual violence in a congregation?* I value our theology of nonviolence and reconciliation. But I offer a caveat on reconciliation when there has been sexual violence and abuse. We cannot rush to reconciliation, asking an abused person to quickly "just forgive and forget." That is way too superficial. It can be theologically abusive. First must come confrontation, then truth-telling, and holding an abuser accountable. The church must be an ally of the abused for this to happen. There must be acknowledgment and confession by the more powerful one. Both the abuser and the abused need time and space for healing. Reconciliation can never be forced or hurried. We might even ask, who is served by the hoped-for reconciliation?

Q13. *Some people seem to long for a return to "tradition" – a time and place supposedly free from divorce when everyone was presumably straight. They may regard the inclusion of sexual diversity in church alongside the normalization of divorce and remarriage as part of the same slippery slope. Are they right to see these things as black-and-white?* No. I don't see a connection between the "inclusion of sexual diversity" and the apparent normalization of divorce and remarriage. This is not permissiveness but rather an acknowledgment of who we are in our diversity, as created in God's image. All of us, whether gay or straight, are equally challenged to live our lives in a Christian way and when we don't quite understand what that way is, we invite the community of faith to help us discern it. Sexual diversity is a necessary feature of congregational life. Let's embrace it and invite God to show us how to live in God's way in our complicated world.

We have learned much about pain within marriages and found some redemptive ways to work through what that might mean. We must always say (along with the Apostle Paul who reminds us — humbly yet boldly — that we see through a glass dimly), that our conclusions must acknowledge our limited understanding and that we need to keep searching for the most redemptive way to live in community and with each other. The slippery slope is the pressure in our society to "commodify" sex.

Q14. *Over the past decade, some influential religious leaders changed their views on the "same-sex" marriage question (Tony Campolo, Michael Coren). Why do you think there is a shift?* First, we have started reading the Bible more carefully. We had assumed that it condemned same-sex marriage when really it doesn't address this issue. It condemns same-sex abuse. And second, we have witnessed same-sex relationships, which were as healthy and life-giving as heterosexual relationships.

Q15. *You state in one of the sermons that you fully affirm the current positions on sexuality by the Mennonite Church (MCUSA/Canada), stemming from 1986 and 1995. Can you explain if and how your view has changed?* I still like much of this statement (as found in the *Confession of Faith in a Mennonite Perspective*, 1995), but not all of it. Under "our covenant," one part reads: "We understand the Bible to teach that sexual intercourse is reserved for a man and a woman united in marriage and that violation of this teaching is a sin. It is our understanding that this teaching also precludes premarital, extramarital, and homosexual activity." This part of the statement seems very dated. I now affirm same-sex marriage. I also recognize that there are many different expressions of physical intimacy, some of which are best limited to a committed relationship. Couples need to communicate with each other their level of commitment and what this means for physical intimacy so that they respect each other's boundaries and grow together into a fuller and deeper love.

A covenant of marriage creates a family unit and opens the possibility for the family circle to include children. Extramarital affairs, as well as abuse within marriage, hurt not only the couple but the larger family circle, especially children. The church's role is to teach responsible sexuality and the beauty of healthy relationships.

Q16. *Why is there still a temptation by Christians to imply sex is evil and to be avoided?* Partly, this may be because some Christians, especially those from churches which are full of warnings about sex, find it difficult to embrace a healthier, more fully-orbed vision of mutuality and respect around sexual expression. This is partly the enduring legacy of patriarchy. The other thing is that we have so many blatant reminders that sex has often been used destructively. We see this in the patterns of violence we associate with sex. We see it used as a weapon in war. We see so many victims of sexual abuse. And, perhaps, people are also afraid of its power over them, due to the potential for erotic addictions. It is hard to embrace and deal with our own desires and our own temptations.

Q17. *In what way do you see the Bible as authoritative?* I like to think that I have been *very* biblical throughout my life as a pastor, not in a closed or dogmatic way, but rather in an open and searching way. I have respect for all people who read the Bible seriously.

I will borrow a metaphor my wife, Lydia, explored in her book, *The Challenge Is in the Naming* (CMU Press, 67-68). Lydia uses the metaphor of the Bible being like our "home." Even when there are things in our home which are dysfunctional, there is a "human-ness" about it (and certainly about each of us), though it is divinely inspired. There are many voices in it, not all singing the same tune. But it is a home where our identity is shaped and where we are inspired to love by a God of love. We see the story of Jesus as being the fulfillment of God's intention for us humans. Our human-ness always tinges our interpretations of Scripture, and yet, we believe that the Spirit of God will gently open our eyes to an even fuller understanding of God's will for us and our world.

Part One
Sex, Love, Intimacy, and Abuse

I knew it would be controversial. Maybe preaching about sex always is. But I hadn't quite prepared myself for this particular broadside. The congregation was already aware, some twenty years ago, that I was advocating for the inclusion of gays in the church. But to do so in a sermon – a biblically-based sermon – was perhaps the last straw for this congregant. "Gary, that is the worst sermon I have ever heard you preach. I am angry." After we both calmed down a bit, we agreed to go golfing together and then sit down over coffee and hash out our differences. And we did. Well, not quite. Neither of us changed our perspective on the church's response to same-sex relationships. But we kept our relationship intact and our respect for each other. And later, when he was dying, he clearly wanted me to pray with him and to conduct his funeral.

There is an old adage about good preaching. It should comfort the afflicted and afflict the "too comfortable." Perhaps occasionally stirring up controversy is part of the preacher's task – as long as there is enough of a trusting relationship with the congregation that healthy dialogue is generated – even if it is heated. I do not see myself as a controversial pastor at all. I have seen myself as a more-or-less traditional Mennonite pastor, steeped in Anabaptism and committed to reading the Bible carefully. And yet, somehow, I have elicited more controversy than I am comfortable with when preaching and writing about human sexuality. There has been sharp critique and challenge to some of the sermons I have preached and articles I have published. Maybe I did hit a nerve sometimes. Maybe I needed to be stretched out of my comfort zone and personality preferences. Maybe controversy is the only way for us to confront the need for change rather than sitting silently in the face of injustice. In my book, *The Pastor-Congregation Duet*, I confess how totally unprepared I was as a young pastor to deal with a story of severe sexual abuse in our community in Lively, Ontario.[1] It did not occur to me that I, as pastor, should have tried to intervene to offer protection to that teenage girl.

I have never been inclined to confront easily or to stir up controversy. I am seen more as a "thoughtful mediator" type, not a "forceful advocate for change." And yet, I have felt "called" to name, confront, and deal honestly with what I saw happening in our context. And I felt challenged to read the Scriptures honestly, trying to make sense of the brutal stories found there. We need to deal with them. Maybe, at its best, reading our Scriptures and reading our world will always provoke controversy and resistance.

And then came the recent stories out of MCEC of clergy sexual abuse. I needed to put my feelings on paper. So, I wrote the following piece, not for publication, but to try to make sense of these stories and what my insides were telling me. It dovetailed with a sermon, which became, 'Painful Musings.'

Part One looks at the spectrum of sexuality, from its many joys of intimacy to the dangers of abuse.

Painful Musings – with Some Hope

Sermon 1: Originally November 8, 1992, revised and expanded in 2023

Psalm 55:12-13; Genesis 1 & 2

> It is not enemies who taunt me — I could bear that; it is not adversaries who deal insolently with me — I could hide from them. But it is you, my equal, my companion, my familiar friend.
>
> Psalm 55:12-13, NRSV

This has been a difficult and painful week for me – maybe for most of us in the Mennonite Church of Eastern Canada (MCEC). Two MCEC pastors and denominational leaders have had their pastoral credentials taken from them for crossing sexual boundaries.

I don't want to raise an accusing finger. I dare to hope that there can be repentance and confession and perhaps even a form of reconciliation. And I need to do my own introspection. Our human sexuality is a wonderful but very complicated thing.

As a retired pastor, I still carry residual pain from the stories shared with me by people, mostly women, who had experienced sexual violence, sometimes from strangers but more often from intimate relationships. Their despair was palpable. I don't think I was always able to respond adequately. There was a high learning curve for us pastors – and for the church. I was inexperienced, naive, and untrained for this reality. But I did try to meet it head-on.

I remind myself that there are two creation stories in Genesis, sitting side by side – both the vision for healthy sexuality and the reality of our brokenness. We all live in both stories. None of us humans fully live out God's vision for healthy sexuality and intimacy. I don't.

The first account of God's creation is the vision for humankind yet the second story is the reality of human experience. The first story breathes a vision for healthy sexuality and mutual intimacy. The second story acknowledges the brokenness lurking at the edge of our intimate relationships. All of us humans live in both stories. We would all have doxologies to offer and confessions to confess. I turn to them and allow my imagination to bring the biblical and contemporary stories together. In those biblical stories, I find hope, vision, and courage for our present-day challenges. In them, I find grist for understanding a healthier vision of our human bodies and of our human sexuality. They are indeed stories worth preaching about.

Genesis 1 & 2 – Stories of Creation

It is all so simple, really, so very, very simple. On the other hand, it is also very complex, so very, very complicated – our sexuality, that is.

The first story. In the beginning, God observed the swirling chaos of earth, the formless void, and said, "My spirit is restless. I've got this creative urge coming over me. I'm going to organize things there on earth, set boundaries, separate day and night, land and sea. And I'm going to create things that have never been. Ah, what possibilities I see in that mess of chaos and darkness."

So, God started organizing and creating. Every once in a while an excited "Wow, that's terrific" rang through the spheres. But when God was almost finished with that mighty surge of awesome creation formation, something was still missing. God was still lonely. "It's wonderful to walk over the face of beautiful earth," thought God, "to listen to the sounds of rivers and storms, to observe all the fascinating creatures I have brought into existence. But I am still lonely. I am a loving being. I am a relating being. I am still incomplete unless I have creatures I can relate to and love. I am who I am, hospitable and loving at the core. A deep part of my being breathes hospitality."

So, God reached deep inside and unleashed the most creative spirit there was, and the image that formed, resembling God's own image, was human. God, in great pleasure and delight, breathed life and spirit into these creatures and laughed with joy. "I have created relating beings," exulted God, "loving beings, male and female beings. Companionship and intimacy can replace loneliness. Hospitality unleashed. This is very, very good. Humans in my image, female and male both fully in my image."

Yes, very good, very simple, and very beautiful in panoramic doxology. Story number one.

But another story also needs to be told, a second telling of this creation account, a more sombre acknowledgment of another reality. This second creation story differentiates between these male and female creatures. This second story paints the reality of brokenness and sinfulness, and it attempts to understand the complexity of human relating. It is a story of ribs and helpmates and forbidden trees and just enough ambiguity to spawn misquotation and "headship" theories. And endless debates between creationists and evolutionists and between those who interpret some Scriptures literally, while others interpret them symbolically. Wouldn't one creation story have been enough, rather than confusing us with two?

"This one shall be called Woman, for out of Man this one was taken," explains the second reading. One could interpret that in many different ways. Never mind — for the moment.

Surely God chuckled when giving these humans genitalia. There is humour in it, isn't there, making a part of the human body that was efficiently dual-purpose and which could not always be controlled by force of will alone. Surely God also laughed with delight at having created a part of the body that gave humans the opportunity to express their deep experience of loving each other intimately. And perhaps God smiled with satisfaction at creating very basic, more or less standard sexual equipment, biologically straightforward and simple, yet emotionally profound and complicated. But then God sighed a deep sigh. Those same organs that could express the intimacy of a loving, caring, deep relationship with another human being could also be used for manipulation, could be used for profit, could be used as a substitute for intimacy, could be used as a game, could be used for abuse, disease, havoc, and for pure lust. Despair and brokenness would result. "Maybe," thought God, "this beautiful gift is too wonderful, too complex, too 'holy' to give to humans. They will only mess it up, make something ugly and cheap out of what is so beautiful."

But really, there was no choice after the idea was

conceived, so to speak, for with sex organs these humans could express a deep love, could express a most intimate caring for each other, and could bring children into their hospitable sphere. These possibilities were too wonderful to give up.

God delighted in seeing Adam and Eve enjoy the Garden of Eden, enjoy each other's companionship, and enjoy conversation with their Creator. These humans tended the garden, named the animals, and ran free and naked and unashamed, taking pleasure in each other's love and in each other's bodies. And God laughed with them in joy. Hospitality utopia.

But alas, other powers also reside in the garden and in each soul. These first humans too had a lust for power. Yes, let's name it. Power. "God knows that when you eat of the fruit of that tree, your eyes will be opened, and you will be like God, knowing good and evil," said the representative of evil. "That fruit is your road to power."

And the rest, as they say, is history. Adam and Eve, as all of us do, yielded to the temptations of power and control over the other, and all chaos broke loose again. The garden was lost. Environmental disaster was on its way. These humans now tried to hide from their Creator, whom they had eagerly conversed with earlier. They now knew the hell of the absence of God from their lives. Adam and Eve blamed each other for their predicament, neither of them wanting to take responsibility for their choices and their actions. Their intimate, free relationship was broken. Alienated from each other, they discovered that their nakedness was now a source of shame, the sex act separated from tender love now devoid of meaning, or even demeaning. So, they sought to cover their genitals with fig leaves, a thing which had not been necessary when they felt close to each other.

In their lust for power, the most powerful lust of all, something was broken in our first parents. The wholeness was gone.

There was a separation taking place between the physical and the spiritual, between body and spirit, between the genitals and the heart. For so many people, sexual intimacy, a form of true hospitality to the one, became instead a false hospitality to the many, making genuine intimacy no longer possible.

We have all been visited by that brokenness. Eden is no more. But we can follow a better vision, a vision more in line with story number one.

We do have to deal with power imbalances. A very skewed reading of the first creation story has traditionally given men power over women. Our Western world has insisted that we "whites" have power over people of colour, that people of wealth have power over people in poverty, and, too often, that males have power over females.

In our current story, we must recognize that pastors have a degree of power over our parishioners – especially if we are male – and that chaplains have power over clients, and theology professors over students. Crossing sexual boundaries is an abuse of power.

But there is another key part to the biblical story of creation. Yes, Adam and Eve lost their innocence and their idyllic garden. But then "The Lord God made garments of skins for the man and for his wife, and clothed them" (Genesis 3:21, NRSV). They were given a second chance – albeit with conditions.

I can't help but think of one further biblical story. King David. Powerful King David. He abuses his power by raping Bathsheba. The king has enormous power; King David totally abuses that power. He would have gotten away with it had it not been for a prophet of God. Nathan. The story starts with these words: "But the thing that David had done displeased the

Lord" (2 Sam 11:27, NRSV). Nathan tells a simple story of a poor man's lamb being stolen by a rich (and powerful) man. King David hears the story and gets angry at that rich man for stealing this poor man's lamb. Nathan uses that story to confront David for his own abuse of power. "You are the man!" And the thing is, David repented. David was not written out of the story of God, out of that history because of his sin. He repented and stayed in the story.

Held accountable. Brought to confession. Stayed in the story. Maybe there is hope for all of us. We all live within this "Adam-Eve" story. On the one hand, there are visions of healthy, life-giving intimacy and loving in it, and on the other hand, an acknowledgment of our human inability to live out that vision fully.

The sermons and articles that follow all grow out of this tension. I make no claims that I have gotten the balance between vision and failure and confession and forgiveness right. But I have tried to deal honestly with the biblical stories.

Stay in the story.

Kissing Frogs – and Other Valentine's Intimacies
Sermon 2: February 09, 2014

Ephesians 2:1-10

I need to begin this sermon with a disclaimer and a warning (maybe even an apology). It is based on a comic, a fairy tale, and a very secular holiday. I will eventually get to the biblical text.

Ah, romance: sweet, mushy, sloppy, sentimental, idealized romance. "Please be my Valentine." When you are in grade three you send that very special Valentine's card to all 30 classmates, fully expecting to get almost as many in return, each claiming that you are "very special."

It never works for Charlie Brown. Valentine's Day is particularly traumatic for him. He sends out his 30 cards and then waits – and waits – at the mailbox. Not a single Valentine comes. Not a single one. If only that little red-haired girl, that very special red-haired girl, would send him one. Charlie Brown waits at that mailbox in vain. His dog Snoopy, who does get a valentine, waits there at the mailbox with him and finally gives him a sloppy lick in the face. Maybe next year.

Saint Valentine, the Catholic priest after whom the day is

named, had a more robust romance in mind. Mind you, the origin of Valentine's Day is still somewhat disputed, so I can pick the story I like best. And what follows is the one I like best.

In the Roman Empire, February 14 was a holiday to honour Juno, the goddess of women and marriage. The following day, February 15, began the "Feast of Lupercalia," a particularly pagan and erotic and sexualized festival.

During the reign of Emperor Claudius the Second, Rome was involved in many very unpopular military campaigns, but far too few Roman men were signing up to fight them. They didn't want to leave wives and lovers behind, only to die in unpopular wars. Claudius had a solution. He cancelled all upcoming engagements and marriages. If these young men didn't have lovers and wives to come home to, maybe they would be more ready to join the army.

A priest by the name of Valentine vehemently objected to this edict. Marriage was ordained by God, he asserted. How could the emperor outlaw marriage just so that he could get more soldiers for his army? So, he secretly officiated marriages for many couples. But one day, he was caught officiating a marriage, and he was condemned to death.

As the story goes, many people visited him in prison – including the daughter of the prison guard. On the day he was to die, the priest Valentine wrote a note to her thanking her for her friendship and loyalty. He signed it, "love, from your Valentine." And then he was beheaded. Later, the church sainted him, and he thus became "Saint Valentine."

From him, we get our Valentine's Day. But there does seem to be a bit of a gap between what he did, and died for, and how the day is seen today. I suppose our Valentine's Day has more affinity with the erotic festival of Lupercalia than it does with a priest secretly officiating Christian weddings.

Yet, there is a deep romance that I hope runs through our

intimate relationships. And there is a very deep romance that runs through the Gospel – the romance of the love of God for each and every one of us.

Ephesians 2 is the Gospel in a nutshell, according to Paul. "But God, who is rich in mercy, out of the great love with which he loved us even when we were dead through our trespasses, made us alive together with Christ" (Eph 2:4-5, NRSV). I love that imagery. "Made us alive together with Christ." Paul continues, "For by grace you have been saved through faith, and this is not your own doing; it is the gift of God – not the result of works, so that no one may boast" (Eph 2:4-10, NRSV). But we are created for good works.

Gathered to hear these words of Paul were both Jewish and gentile believers. The Jewish ones were tempted to believe that their heritage, their keeping of the laws, and their good works earned them good standing with God. The gentile believers found it hard to believe that God could love them without their earning that love.

The deep truth of this well-known text from Ephesians is that all humans need a saviour. The deep truth is that we cannot save ourselves by keeping laws or doing good works. The deeper truth is that only God can save us. God does so by loving us. But in return, we are expected to do "good works." But we are not saved by our good works. We are saved by God's powerful love.

This is the sermon in a nutshell. The rest is only application. I might be wise to simply stop my sermon right here. But I really did want to get to that famous German fairy tale yet. There is a version embellished a bit by Wes Seeliger, where he gets poetic and playful with the image of kissing a frog. He asks us to consider with whom we identify in this fairy tale.

Wes Seeliger[1] described how we sometimes get "the frog feeling," unable to do what we wish we could do. We end up "on a lily pad floating down the great river of life...too froggish to budge." Knowing that feeling we all have at times, we can now re-imagine the fairy tale, feeling ugly and also despairing that "cute chicks" don't generally kiss frogs. But, in the fairy tale, that does happen, and the spell cast on the prince by the wicked witch is broken.

I wonder with whom you identify in the fairy tale. I think we are meant to identify mostly with the frog, the one feeling down. Or do we identify with the princess, with the one trying to lift that person up?

But one caveat in our world, a big caveat: We do need to recognize that there are wicked witches out there, predators of one kind or another. These are the predatory kissers. Even sometimes in the church. In our world, we do need to give out warnings about abusive kissing. But this is a fairy tale. We will take it as a metaphor, a metaphor for true love, the kind of God-like love that transforms and heals. So in Seelieger's application, the role of the church is to "kiss frogs."

Self-worth

The issue for the prince – and for many of us – was feeling froggish, feeling low, feeling ugly, lacking self-worth, lacking self-esteem. I suspect that most of us feel the tension between feeling like a frog – maybe only sometimes, maybe even most times – and feeling like a prince or princess – at least occasionally. Most of us struggle most of our lives with claiming a healthy sense of self-worth. It is when we feel bad about ourselves that we are most likely to have relationship issues with the people we love. It is when we feel bad about ourselves that we are likely to act out in damaging ways. It is when we feel bad about ourselves that we are at risk of getting caught in addictive and abusive behaviours.

And yet, healthy self-esteem is hard to come by. We assume that if we work harder, we can earn self-esteem – if we would only study harder and longer – if we would practice our instrument more – if we would really be successful at something, anything. We try so hard. We develop self-improvement projects – surely, they will improve our poor self-image. We work harder. We strive to get better grades in school. We buy new clothes. We accumulate possessions, or boyfriends, or girlfriends. We try to improve our looks through cosmetics, exercise, or surgery. We practice extra hard at our sport. Surely if I become a sports hero or music all-star, I will be loved!

There we are, on a sinking lily pad, taking croaking lessons, competing in the jumping Olympics, having wart augmentation surgery, getting another degree in fly-catching, and buying up more lily pads. But nothing seems to help. Because everything heroic or cosmetic only gives a temporary boost to our self-esteem, but it does not permanently change how we feel inside. Inside, change comes only from being loved – loved as we are, accepted as we are, warts and all. Only a "kiss" will do it.

Listen carefully again to our text. "But God, who is rich in mercy, out of the great love with which he loved us even when we died through our trespasses, made us alive together with Christ..." Made us alive together with Christ. What a great image. What a wonderful definition of salvation. The emptiness inside is filled. Life bubbles over with energy, vitality, and love. Made alive.

There we were – a demoralized frog on a lily pad in a smelly swamp. And one day, royalty came along, the God of the puckered lips in the guise of a beautiful princess – and gave us a big smack right on our ugly lips – with a crash, a boom and a zap. A kiss, just when we were feeling un-kissable. A kiss, a great big smacker, and the metamorphosis began.

The Bible says this over and over again. God loves you. God loves me. Period. No qualifications. God loves us. Know it. Feel it. Experience it deeply at the core of your being.

Application

Ah, the God of the puckered lips is on a "kissing" expedition. Having kissed us and turned us from frogs into princes and princesses, God invites us to join the "kissing army."

God has a whole army of puckered lips out there. This army doesn't go about pouring insecticide into the swamp trying to get rid of the frogs. It doesn't go about telling everyone how froggish they really are. Everyone knows that already. They point instead to the possibility of being princes and princesses. Their job is to love, to affirm, to encourage, to value, and to make others feel special. They even risk "kissing" someone with smelly breath.

I think this needs to start at home.

You spouses – be true Valentines to each other at home. Kiss each other often, in spite of smelly breath, and especially when the other feels froggish. We so easily become experts in finding fault with each other. It so easily happens that we start to major in complaints and criticism after a long marriage. No one needs to put on better makeup to offer a simple kiss. And we so easily forget that our spouse, like we ourselves, can only live with joy by being repeatedly kissed and affirmed and told that they are deeply loved.

Parents — you have the sacred privilege and duty to be the primary "kissing" agents for your children as they grow up. Don't allow a negative atmosphere in your home. Don't major in criticizing and reproving your children. Of course, there must be guidelines and rules and discipline. These are part of a genuine love. But far more importantly, there needs to be constant affirmation, constant building up, constant loving, constant offers of kisses. Otherwise, they may not be able to turn into the beautiful princesses and princes that they were created to be.

Children – don't be too "cool" to show and express your love for your parents. Someday if you become a parent, you may be offering kisses to your child and hoping they accept them! Parents can also feel down and discouraged and overwhelmed, and they also need to be told they are loved by you.

Grandparents – what an incredible gift your grandchildren are to you. And what a gift you can be to them. See their beauty, not their blemishes. Gift them constantly with your unconditional love.

Single people in the church – I hope you know that you are valued, appreciated, and loved for who you are. Your worth is intrinsic and not dependent on being married – on having a spouse. You are such an important part of God's kissing army.

But remember, we must all ask others for consent when offering our kisses, respecting their dignity and decision to not accept our offer of kisses. It is not okay to take away their choice, to silence the other, or to major in criticizing.

I think Saint Valentine would approve. He risked beheading to bless couples getting married.

The church is a gathering of God's kissing army. From our Ephesians text, we hear again that God loves us, and we reaffirm our love for God – and our love for each other. Loving each other does not mean always agreeing with each other. In fact, within a loving family – and church – it is quite okay to disagree with each other and to challenge each other, and to discuss and debate and even confront each other and sometimes to get upset or angry. These are all okay.

What is not okay is to take away the dignity of the other, to silence the other, to major in criticizing, belittling, or avoiding the other. Doing so will risk turning the other back into a frog.

We are all just in the process of turning into princes and princesses – and could easily revert to feeling froggish if pushed in that direction. By being invited into God's kissing army, we have the amazing privilege and calling to build each other up, to affirm each other, and to help each other uncover the image of God within each one of us.

And then there are our neighbours, our co-workers, our classmates, the people who serve us, and the people we serve – many of them needing a "kiss" rather than a rebuke.

"Beloved, since God loved us so much, we also ought to love one another."

So, what is the task of the church? TO KISS FROGS, of course.

"With love, from your Valentine."

Shelter in a Time of Storm –
Sexual Abuse
Sermon 3: April 23, 1989

Psalm 55; Matthew 25:34-36

I first saw "Graeta" from a bit of a distance. She had come to our church to see the secretary, not the pastor. When I entered the church and approached the office, Graeta hurried away, a two-year-old son in tow, careful to avoid meeting my eyes. She had moved into an apartment not too far from the church only a few months earlier. Our secretary looked approachable, so one afternoon when Graeta noticed that my car was not at the church, she came to the church to "look around," and maybe to chat with the secretary.

It took a lot of courage for Graeta to finally risk coming into my office some days later. She said she was a Mennonite who came from another city. But her husband, also a Mennonite church member, did not want her to go to church. She acknowledged that they were having a few marriage problems, though "nothing serious." He did not want her to leave the apartment while he was gone. She just wanted to look inside the church and maybe sit awhile in the sanctuary.

Graeta came to the church a few more times, once with bruises on her face. Finally, she had the courage to meet my eyes. "I'm afraid of men," she said in a high, unnatural voice. She was 19 years old. She had been married for a year and a half. It had seemed to the church secretary that she treated her son rather roughly.

One day, she came to the church very agitated and burst out, "I'm afraid for my son. I'm afraid for myself. My husband is out of control. He is threatening us." Our secretary took mother and son to a woman's shelter.

That evening, "Hannes" called, very angrily, demanding I tell him where his wife and son were. She had "run away," and he accused me of helping her. I responded, "From what I understand, you have abused your wife and your son. They need protection from you. I will not tell you where they are. I will welcome you to come see me." "We just had a little argument," responded Hannes, "nothing serious at all."

Over the weeks, Hannes called a few more times. Finally, he was ready to meet with me, though, it seemed to me, only to get access to his wife. Over the next months, I heard the story from both wife and husband several more times. The pattern was familiar. The tension would build at home. Hannes would try to control every move Graeta made, not letting her go shopping alone, visit a friend, or to do anything without his permission. Graeta would try her best not to upset him. But some little thing would trigger a violent rage, and he would beat her and their son. Then he would feel terribly sorry, would profess his love for them, and would promise never to do it again. And in a few weeks, the pattern would repeat itself.

Hannes and Graeta had married at 17 years of age. Both had been abused by their fathers. Hannes' father, seldom home, often took a heavy belt to his son "just to discipline him as he ought." He often told his son, "You are no good. All you do is cause us trouble. I've got to beat the evil out of you." Graeta's father was given to violent rages. Graeta could never please her father, no matter how hard she tried. He criticized her constantly. Often, he beat her. Neither Hannes nor Graeta had a strong sense of personal value and self-worth.

Both of their fathers were very religious and were very strict. They both insisted that giving strong discipline was their religious duty. They would recite – "Spare the rod and spoil the child" – "Children, obey your parents." Apparently, they did not read further in Ephesians 6, where it says, "Fathers, do not provoke your children to anger." Both fathers insisted that they were just fulfilling their Christian duty of being "the head of the house."

Hannes and Graeta both acknowledged that they got married to escape home. But they couldn't escape the scars and the pain of their upbringing, and they carried these into their marriage and into their parenting. "The anger just builds up," said Hannes, "and I can't control it. I feel powerless. And suddenly it explodes. I don't mean to beat Graeta. I love her. I just can't help myself." And Graeta says the same thing when she beats their son.

The cycle of violence continues into the next generation.

"Jessie" came into my office and said, "I think I can trust you. I think you will believe me. You let your wife preach at our church." Jessie's husband was a very respected member of the community and of her church. He was a High School principal. And he regularly beat his wife and degraded her sexually. One day, Jessie came home and found her husband in the act of having intercourse with their adolescent daughter.

Later, Jessie wrote me a letter. "This molten anger within me will only harden to hatred if it has no positive release and dispersal, but the mere thought, let alone a confirmation, makes me feel a rage that will either destroy me or him or will move the whole rotten morass into the sea and it is very, very scary. I feel like an ant at the foot of the Rockies, and how is even an ant with anger going to move it? Or is it only a mushy mountain of stench and manure? Can I really carry this rot, a little piece at a time, to the sea?"

Jessie's husband just laughed at her. "No one will believe you. You are nobody." Jessie asked me, "Should I charge him and take him to court? But if I do that, what will happen to my daughter?"

Family Violence

What is family violence? How do we define family abuse? Judith Dyck gives this helpful definition:[1]

> Domestic violence includes child abuse, spouse abuse, or elder abuse. It can include sexual abuse involving incest, marital rape or any sexual behaviour that is tricked or forced. It can include psychological abuse involving the systematic destruction of the victims' self-esteem through harassment, deprivation, name-calling, constant criticism, isolation from friends and relatives, or destruction of pets or property. It can include neglect on the part of a caretaker, which leads to emotional trauma, physical injury, or death. Whatever the type, family violence creates enormous pain and suffering for those involved in it.

What is the magnitude of the problem of family violence? This question is almost impossible to answer. Most family violence does not get reported. And yet, it is very common. Within the past several years, I have collected reams of material, papers, and stories. For the 1980s we have statistics about the shocking frequency of abuse. Generally, one out of every three girls and one out of every seven boys will be sexually abused by the age of 18. At least half of all child sexual abuse occurs within the family. About 20% of children are abused at home.

In Canada, experts have estimated that one out of every ten women is abused. Yet many researchers feel that this figure is far too conservative and that the real numbers are far higher. They say that 95% of the abusers are men and that perhaps 5% of husbands are abused by their wives.[2]

There is a growing realization that many aged parents are being abused by their children. We are just now becoming aware of the enormity of this problem.

Does abuse happen in church circles too? Do Christians abuse each other? Does it happen within the Mennonite Church with its theology of peace and non-violence? Yes, it does. All the studies indicate that the rate of abuse is just as high within the church as outside the church and that it happens within the Mennonite Church as frequently as any place else. Many abusive husbands and fathers justify their abuse by basing it on their God-given right to be head of the family. Abuse is more likely to happen in families that are highly structured and authoritarian.

> It is not enemies who taunt me – I could bear that; it is not adversaries who deal insolently with me – I could hide from them. But it is you, my equal, my companion, my familiar friend. Psalm 55:12-13, NRSV

Who is the Abuser?

What is the profile of the abuser? It may surprise us that those who abuse their spouse or their children may not seem like bad people but are some of the nicest people you know. They come from every cultural, ethnic, and religious origin. They come from every social class – rich, poor, or middle class. It is no respecter of education or vocation. They are doctors, lawyers, labourers, electricians, professors – ministers. But they do have much in common.

They are part of the violence that runs throughout our society, a violence in which women and children are most often the victims. Men are socialized to be strong, independent, aggressive, and competitive. They think they are supposed to take charge and be in control. They are supposed to suppress emotions – except for anger. The man is the boss. Sex is seen either as a conquest or as a reward for being strong. Each one of us carries a shadow side of violence within. I know it is within me. Several times, I have spanked my children out of anger, not love, more for my sake than for theirs. And in that, I have abused them.

According to various studies, there are several common traits shared by people who abuse their power. It helps us to identify factors and patterns so we can increase awareness that these traits may lead to violence. While it may seem counter-intuitive, abusers often have low self-esteem and they become very guarded when someone wants to get emotionally close. They often lack coping skills when facing frustration, conflict or stress, often because they came from homes where violence was used to deal with struggles for power, and they quickly become jealous and controlling, making unreasonable demands of those close to them.

Quite often they will espouse traditional gender role expectations, believing they are the boss, that the man should be head of the home, and insist they have the final say in all decisions, particularly with finances and will make threats, whether direct or indirect, aiming for others to remain dependent upon them rather than allow them independence.

They will even invade the privacy of others, yet remain rather secretive about their own life, schedule, and communications with others. They are eager to deny or belittle any abusive actions or behaviours and choose to lie or speak in misleading ways about their intent, sometimes insisting that they are in fact the victim. They typically lack empathy and seek to blame others.

Their abuse of others is, by their account, never their own fault. "She drove me to it." "She had it coming." Their ego is too fragile to accept personal responsibility for their anger. We are told that 9 out of 10 abusers do not believe anything is wrong and do not accept that they need to change.

Their only solution is a violent response to these feelings. The pattern is almost always the same – tension builds up, there is an explosion, and then there is remorse and promises and gentleness. But there is no real repentance, no real change. The cycle repeats itself.

Why do men abuse their wives and children? Because it works to control members of their family. And it works to numb their own inner feelings.

What happens to the abused person? What is the pain? Abused people may lose their sense of self-esteem. Women have often been socialized to be meek and submissive, to take the servant role within the family system, and to accept the status that others give to them. It is hard to value yourself as a person if someone is using you as a punching bag. Sexually abused women may feel humiliated and ashamed of their bodies. They may become angry and resentful about sex because they associate sex with power and control, not with love. They may also be afraid of further hurt, which may cause them to "give in" so as not to provoke another outburst.

They may feel guilty in a perverse way, internalizing the taunts of the abuser. They may feel so trapped and frustrated and depressed that they may engage in self-destructive behaviour.

Psalm 55 - As Lament

Psalm 55 was written by a person who felt abused by someone "close." It was "not an enemy" or "adversary who deals insolently with me" but "you, my equal, my companion, my familiar friend." It is thought that these words were written by King David after his son Absalom rebelled against him. The son has abused his father. The words reflect the pain and confusion experienced when someone you trust and love turns against you. We remember, though, that it was King David who raped Bathsheba.

The lament continues. "My heart is in anguish within me; the terrors of death have fallen on me. Fear and trembling have beset me; horror has overwhelmed me" (Psalm 55:4-5, NRSV). The confusion and pain come because of broken trust. "But it is you, a man like myself, my companion, my close friend, with whom I once enjoyed sweet fellowship at the house of God, as we walked about among the worshipers... My companion attacks his friends; he violates his covenant. His talk is smooth as butter, yet war is in his heart; his words are more soothing than oil, yet they are drawn swords" (Psalm 55:13-14, 20-21, NRSV).

The betrayal is overwhelming. The writer longs for escape. For many women and children, there is no alternative but to escape. Nothing else will stop the abuse.

O that I had wings like a dove! I would fly away and be at rest; truly, I would flee far away, I would lodge in the wilderness, I would hurry to find a shelter for myself from the raging wind and tempest. Psalm 55:6-8, NRSV

Abused people need a shelter. They need a shelter in the time of violent storms.

Intervention: How can the church respond?

Break the silence. Family violence is a topic which we in the church have been very slow to address. We need to break the silence. We need to expose the problem. We need to make it safe for abused persons to come forward. We need to say that we will take abuse seriously. The church needs to be a shelter for persons experiencing abuse.

Listen to the victim. Many victims will say, "The slow, painful healing process began when someone listened to me, when they finally believed me." We have not wanted to listen. We have not wanted to believe. "Maybe the problem will simply go away." We need to listen to the stories of those who have been abused, to listen to more than just the words. And listen also to the pain they are experiencing.

Intervene so that the abuse stops, which starts with listening. It may continue with providing protection, shelter, and support. It may mean putting victims in touch with community resources, shelters, support groups, and counselling. Don't let the abuse continue. We will make a big mistake if we say what the church has too often said – that the abused person should stay in an abusive context because it is her Christian duty. The best hope for an abusive relationship is "separation" (temporary at first), so that the abuse stops and so that basic issues can be dealt with.

Don't blame the victim. There is often already enough self-blame. Too often, the church has tried to justify the abuser. If someone gets raped, we ask what she was wearing. We say – "Men are like that when they get aroused." Put the blame where it belongs – on the abuser. There is never any excuse at all for forcing your way, physically or sexually, on anyone. Being drunk is not an excuse. There is no justification.

Confront the abuser. We cannot look the other way. We know that abusers will absolutely deny they did anything wrong. Nine out of ten abusers do not believe that they need to end their hurtful behaviours. They see nothing wrong with what they do. We need to tell them that it is wrong, absolutely wrong. They need to learn that they can be angry without having to hit or lash out. Violence is a learned reaction to stress and it can be unlearned. But that is very difficult. The prognosis is not very good. Most of us resist personal change. Most abusers will take counselling only when ordered to by the courts, and they will discontinue as soon as legally possible. We do not easily change, no matter how many promises we make.

Prevention

The church must also work on the prevention of violence. The church can provide education and modelling for healthy, loving, violence-free relationships and can offer problem-solving and conflict-resolution skills. The church can say that it is quite okay, and very normal, to get angry, but it is not okay to abuse someone when we are angry. We can educate ourselves to respect each other so much that we will never violate another person – especially not those we love.

Part of this preventive education may be to re-interpret our theology of male-female relationships. Any theology which assumes that the male is the boss is wide open to being used to justify abuse. We need to apply our theology of peace to the domestic sphere and to our intimate relationships. We need to take away any props which justify abuse – or justify non-intervention in abuse. The message of Jesus is always about love – unconditional love. It is about freedom, respect, and dignity.

Afterword

"Jessie" wrote, "You can't know the impact that sermon on the bent-over woman had on me at deep, deep levels. The image of Christ defending her and declaring her validity and personhood irrespective of the hierarchies – something moved in me below the emotions and in the base of my soul."

Perhaps, if we provide shelter for persons caught in a storm of abuse, we will hear the words of Jesus, paraphrased just a little:

> I was raped, and you stood by me,
>> I was abused, and you sheltered me,
>> I was violated, and you intervened.
>> Matthew 25:34-36

In the Image of God
Sermon 4: November 29, 1992

Philippians 2:1-11

Last summer at the Mennonite General Conference sessions in Sioux Falls, U.S., we spent quite a bit of time discussing and debating a resolution on violence and sexual abuse. The original resolution was put forward by a group of men who said that we men have to take responsibility for much of the violence and abuse inflicted on women and that we men have to work to put an end to it.

The debate was vigorous. I spoke to it several times, and, as many of you read, my name was mentioned in our Mennonite papers, quoting me saying that I thought patriarchy was sin. There it was, all over North America: *Pastor Gary Harder from Toronto says that patriarchy is sin.* I have received quite a bit of heat for that "opinion-conviction," some of the heat coming from here at Toronto United Mennonite Church, where I am the pastor. So, I thought that this morning I might as well jump right into the fire and explain why I think patriarchy is sinful. (Anyone bring a fire extinguisher?) Any discussion of human sexuality isn't complete unless we struggle with the systemic issues involved. At Sioux Falls, the debate focused on this question: Is sexual abuse only the individual sin of a sinful individual, or is there a larger systemic problem which fosters violence and abuse?

Last weekend, I was in Saskatoon to speak at the Ministers and Deacons conference. I stayed in the home of old friends who are the Conference Pastors for the Saskatchewan Mennonite Conference. They had some really heavy stuff to deal with – two cases of sexual misconduct involving church leaders. In one case, an ordained lay minister had sexually abused a child over a period of many years. Another church leader, not ordained, had been under observation by police for a number of years for frequenting prostitutes. Are these two church leaders just two particularly sinful individuals, or is there something about the way our society – and church – views males and females which contributed to their sexual deviancy?

I personally believe that patriarchy is a system that contributes to violence and sexual abuse.

Patriarchy, Sexism, and Paternalism

I want to try to give some definitions so that we can be a little more precise about what we mean.

Patriarchy

In its narrow sense, patriarchy is defined by people like Sandra Schneiders and Rosemary Radford Ruether as a social system based on men's absolute power over women. They say that the structures of society have been mostly structured by men and have entrenched male power – governments, legal systems, systems of work, education, the church, the home. It took until this century for Canada — in 1929 — to declare that women were indeed human. That there was a need to declare that women were fully human speaks volumes.

Patriarchy has to do with the assumption that males are superior to females, have more value, and deserve to have a "God-given" power over them. It is a divinely established right granted by God and upheld by the Bible. The man is head of the house. Women must be silent in church. Any rebellion against this system is a rebellion against God.

In its broader sense, patriarchy has to do with a system of hierarchical power over others; power is based not on choice or gifts or mutual agreement but on some assumed inherent superiority. There is a basic principle at play – it is the subordination of females to males, of one race to the other, of poor to the rich, of children to adults, of believers to clergy. Ruether says, "not only the subordination of females to males, but the whole structure of Father-ruled society: aristocracy over serfs, masters over slaves, kings over subjects, racial overlords over colonized people."[1] It includes racism, ageism, classism, colonialism, clericalism, as well as sexism.[2]

I think all of this is sinful.

The structures of patriarchy are changing in our society – but amidst great upheaval. The systems that encode male superiority are breaking down, though there is great resistance. Outcomes in our courts are changing. Workplaces are changing. Some churches are even changing. Societal understandings of the roles of men and women are changing. What is not changing quickly enough, however, are the attitudes and presuppositions deeply lodged within each of us. "Sexism" will not quickly disappear.

Sexism

Sexism is the self-understanding of us males that we are the superior sex and females the inferior sex. We men have more power. We are the prime decision-makers. It is the self-understanding that males are the aggressive ones, the ones who lead out. At its worst, this justifies violence when we men "conquer" females or try to control females, who, after all, are there to serve men. It justifies "date rape" because, after all, that is what men are like. Sexism is socializing men to be aggressive and to exercise control and power over women and socializing women to be passive and seductive and serving men.

Both patriarchy and sexism cause immense pain for both men and women. Women because they are so often abused, violated, demeaned, and denied their rightful place. Men because they are so often isolated and alone and stuck in roles, attitudes, and relationships that destroy their souls. I would name both patriarchy and sexism as sinful – that is, they are not what God intends. They are a violation of God's vision when God created males and females.

Paternal

Another word needs discussion – paternal. Paternalism has a negative connotation, a kind of benign patriarchy. But "paternal" need not have a negative connotation. Paternal and maternal primarily mean "parental." One can be parental without exorcising absolute power over one's children. One can be a father or mother in a nurturing way which respects and affirms a child.

I think we need to reclaim a healthy vision of what it means to be male and what it means to be female. Something seems so wrong with the way things are. There is such enormous pain in the way things are. There is so much dysfunction. There is so much violence, abuse, and despair. There is so much guilt and loss of identity for men. There is such a denial of true personhood for women. Can we find a new vision?

Let's carry these definitions back to the biblical stories to see how they can be applied in life-giving ways.

Incarnation

In Genesis, we read that God created humans in his own image – created us male and female. The text suggests that we humans were wonderfully made.

In the New Testament, we read about the coming of Jesus, the one who carried the full divine image of God. This Jesus was both fully divine and fully human. In his "humanness," we can see a vision of what it means to be fully human – whether male or female.

Today is the first Sunday of Advent. In Advent, we prepare to celebrate the coming of God among us in the form of Jesus. We call it "Incarnation" – God becoming human. God living with us. What did Jesus show us about being "human"?

Philippians 2

Listen to the Christ hymn in Philippians 2 – a total contrast to patriarchy, an absolute contrast to "over/under" relationships. It reads as an absolute contrast to assumptions of power and privilege for some. If anyone had the divine right to power and privilege, it was Jesus, the Son of God. The Christ Hymn is a shocking alternative vision.

> Let the same mind be in you that was in Christ Jesus,
> who, though he was in the form of God, did not regard
> equality with God as something to be exploited, but
> emptied himself, taking the form of a slave, being born
> in human likeness. And being found in human form, he
> humbled himself and became obedient to the point of
> death – even death on a cross.
> Phil 2:5-8, NRSV

God, the all-powerful one, came to earth in the form of Jesus, the Son, as a fully-human male, a sexual being. One who lived out a new male identity, one separated from domination, violence, exploitation, and privilege. In his human form, Jesus lived out the divine image.

Jesus knew himself to be in the form of God. He knew himself to have the power of God. But he made the choice not to exploit this equality, this power. Rather, he chose to "empty himself," to take on full humanity, with all the human limitations implied. And he chose not to cling to the privileges and powers of male humanity. He chose to be a loving servant.

Jesus was not a weak person. He was not a wimp. He was not a doormat for everyone to step on. He was incredibly strong, self-assured, and clear about who he was. He confronted people who needed confrontation. He challenged those who abused their power. He continued to have great personal power. But he emptied himself of its coercive nature.

Having said all this, I want to register one strong note of caution. It is one thing to hear this servant hymn as one who holds power, is tempted to exploit that power, and generally lives from a position of privilege. It is quite another to hear this hymn when feeling exploited and powerless. It is not a call for further self-abasement for those who already feel themselves to be doormats to the more privileged.

We do need to remember that Jesus chose to empty himself of coercive power. He could do so because he knew himself to be a valued person, created in the image of God, worthy of respect, called and loved by God.

Jesus did not give up his power. He continued to have enormous power – power for healing, for loving, and for challenging persons and institutions. What he gave up was coercive power. He gave up privilege. He gave up any superiority of class or culture or position or gender.

The New Possibilities in Being Male and Being Female

When we look at the kind of humanness Jesus modelled, I think we can see many new possibilities for being male and female. We see a whole new vision for healthy, life-giving relationships between men and women. Jesus defined being male differently than his society did – or our society. He repudiated coercive power, and any kind of domination, control, aggression or violence. In their place, Jesus affirmed true humility, peacemaking, non-violence, and respectful, caring human relationships.

In these ways, Jesus challenged both men and women to conversion. He challenged men to abandon their assumption of human superiority over women, and he challenged women to value the traits which their society claimed made them inferior to men. He called both men and women to follow him and to call out the good news of God's reign.

Jesus modelled something very new in the way he related to women. In story after story, he relates to women in a respectful way, which gives them dignity and worth.

- He chose women to be his disciples, his followers. This was very counter-cultural.
- As a rabbi, a teacher, he included women among his students (Luke 10:39). He gave them dignity by teaching them, which was not the norm in that world.
- He healed a widow's son (Luke 7:11-17), praised their faith (Matt 9:22), and accepted their love (Luke 7:37-38).
- He defended women against arbitrary divorce (Matt 19:3-9).

- Jesus had friendships of various levels of intimacy with women. It was said of Mary and Martha that he had a relationship of genuine friendship and love with them.
- Three women, Mary Magdalene, Mary the mother of James, and Salome, were the first persons to witness his resurrection, and they were the ones called to tell the rest of the disciples that he was indeed alive (Mark 16).

From the biblical record, we assume that Jesus chose to be single and celibate in a society that mostly precluded giving any dignity or social standing to anyone not married. Jesus chose celibacy, not because sex is bad or evil or because marriage itself is somehow secondary, but because he could best fulfil his ministry and his vision that way. In my opinion, Jesus could as well have been married and been sexually active.[3]

But he didn't marry. You can be a complete and whole human being without marriage and the accompanying sex. In fact, we all need to learn to be single and complete before we can be "coupled" in a healthy way. Singleness is okay. It is affirmed. Jesus didn't need to have a spouse, sexual partner, and children to be fully human.

Afterword

What are we left with? We live in a society which is still very patriarchal and sexist. But we have a Christ story and a Christ hymn which provide an alternative vision of male-female relationships.

This Advent season, I invite you to sing a new song of incarnation. It is a song of mutuality, of respect, of empowering each other, and of true intimacy. I invite us all, in our singing, to reject all hurtful sexual games – all notions of conquest or manipulation or pressuring people to do what they don't want to do.

I invite us to reject any sense of superiority and the exercise of power based on our gender.

I invite young people to make their goal, not sexual conquest, or scoring, but rather becoming the kind of person who can sustain honest, caring, respectful relationships.

I invite single persons to know that personal wholeness and dignity are much more basic to their lives than whether or not they have a sexual partner.

I invite married couples to the kind of loving, intimate relationship where sexual expression is never forced but always the gift of joyful, intimate knowing.

I invite the congregation as a congregation to also be "self-emptying" and to refuse to exercise power over people. Always, we must sing invitations to be Christ-like.

Sing a song of incarnation, a Christ hymn, a celebration of true maleness and femaleness in the image of God.

A Postscript on Patriarchy (1993)

I preached this sermon in 1992 at TUMC and then published an edited and shorter version in *Mennonite Reporter* on May 23, 1993. That piece must have been somewhat controversial and was sharply critiqued (July 12, 1993) by a Mennonite scholar, Walter Klaassen, whom I have a great deal of respect for, challenging me for trying to be "politically correct." Here are some excerpts from that challenge.

> "Father" is today a politically incorrect word. We make patriarchy into a synonym of oppression and then condemn it as sin. What has happened to careful and responsible thought among Christians?... Christians cannot make patriarchy into a sin without calling into question some main supports of the biblical story. Clearly, the God of Abraham, Isaac, and Jacob is the worst of sinners because he exercised his patriarchal power by punishing and abusing his child Israel... The biblical language about God, especially in the New Testament, is fatherhood language... It is frustrating to

see Christians so thoughtlessly adopting the rules of political correctness without being aware of how judgmental it is.

Walter Klaassen

Foolish that I am, I responded with another piece challenging that critique (*Mennonite Reporter,* July 12, 1993):

"Political correctness" is indeed an issue Christians urgently need to address. I agree with Klaassen that popular trends of superficial and deadly moralism should have no rootage in Christian faith.

I also think that Klaassen misses the central issue raised by my critique of patriarchy – the pain of women and the pain of men resulting from structures in society which imply power and superiority of half of created humanity over the other half.

I am not a linguist and cannot defend my definition of patriarchy in linguistic terms. I have used it as some women theologians define it. If we stumble over the word, let us at least recognize that language is dynamic and that meanings change.

It is a powerful thing to be able to define words. The privilege of doing so should include all who are affected by our language use. I speak as a pastor who regularly hears the pain of persons affected negatively by dominance, which is often supported by language defined by males.

The charge of simply trying to be politically correct is significant if the church is only following the winds of fashion – as it too often does. But that charge also, particularly in the present case, trivializes the immense pain so many people experience and

serves as a justification for continuing male superiority.

The critique of a system which gives inherent
rights because of sex, class or race has a much more
potent core than political correctness. I find it in the
scriptures and in the Christian faith.

Of course, the Scriptures are not unambiguously
clear on these issues. Biblical people lived in a strong
patriarchal context, and it is not surprising that that
context is reflected in the record of encounters with
each other and with God....

In the cases of violence and slavery, one can find
voices in the scriptures which seem to justify them as
God's will. But there is a movement of clarification
throughout the Scriptures, culminating in the prophets,
and especially in Jesus, which clearly affirms that God's
will for us is the rejection of violence and of structures
which enslave people.

The peace churches have been at the forefront of
the Christian voice on these two issues. Why can't we
be at the forefront in affirming equality and mutuality
between males and females?

Klaassen lumps patriarchy and fatherhood
together, intimating that separating them is an arbitrary
violation of language. Then he can say that since the
biblical language about God is fatherhood language, it
follows that patriarchy supports the biblical story and,
therefore, cannot be criticized.

To me, this is a violation of language. I embrace
fatherhood language for God – as long as it is not the
only language I use for God. We do believe that God is
beyond gender, though both male and female images
help us understand something of who God is.

I embrace my own fatherhood as a wonderful and sacred privilege, though sometimes I have abused it by exercising selfish power over my children. I embrace my maleness, though sometimes I struggle with what it means to be in the image of God.

But I do not embrace a system which allows and even encourages male dominance and superiority.

Klaassen also justifies patriarchy by referring to Old Testament stories, which can be interpreted as God punishing and abusing his child, Israel. A series of issues need to be dealt with here.

Is there such an automatic connection between males and a supposedly male God that allows males on earth to imitate God punishing Israel?

Surely God is sovereign and can treat Israel as God deems appropriate. But in the O.T. record, we have huge issues of interpretation to work through before we name the punishing actions of God as a justification of patriarchy here on earth.

There are also questions about how we understand the punishment of God. In the case of war and violence, Mennonites have asked whether every word directing violence is an indication of the will/words of God or if it is better interpreted as the understanding of the people of God at a given time.

Regardless of our hermeneutics here, the primary picture we have of God is given by Jesus (though this picture differs only in clarity from that of the Hebrew Scriptures). And just as this Jesus clarifies the will of God regarding violence, so this Jesus clarifies the will of God regarding male-female relationships.

No, Jesus did not crusade against patriarchy (or against slavery or even against war), but he lived and taught a new possibility for both males and females. In this is salvation.

A final plea. Let all of us males who talk about issues such as patriarchy include as our conversation partners women as well as men. My plea is to converse with both women who have experienced abuse because of being female (there are many in our congregations) and women who are doing biblical and theological work around these issues.

Not to do so is both arrogant and, well, patriarchal.

Part Two
Sexuality in Story, Poetry, and Song

This set of sermons is simply based on biblical stories – stories of sex, love, intimacy, power, and abuse. They are a collection of sermons preached over a number of years. I never set out to preach a "series of sermons" on sex. But, the challenges of contemporary life at any given time in my ministry drew me to these texts and these stories. The Bible deals rather straightforwardly with the wide scope of human sexual experience – from the beautiful to the abusive, from genuine intimacy to exploitive violence. These stories offer perspective, warning, challenge, and hope for our struggles to deal with exploitive sex in our day and to offer glimpses of the beauty and profound intimacy of healthy sexuality.

Starting with "stories" rather than with "commandments and warnings" is a choice I make. Stories invite us into human experience and offer glimpses of both the beautiful and the painful in living out our lives as sexual beings. They invite us to identify with the characters and thus allow self-reflection and perhaps confession. Beginning with commandments and warnings and rules (for example, the Ten Commandments) can put us into a defensive mode, not as open to the beauty of how God created us.

The Bible itself starts with stories, both in the Old Testament and in the New Testament. The power of stories seems to me to be a good starting place for exploring human sexuality in all of its multiple, complicated, and beautiful manifestations in our lives.

A Symphony of Sensuality
Sermon 5: February 9, 2003

Song of Songs

The Song of Songs, a book in the Bible, has had a troublesome history. You see, it is not particularly religious, God is not mentioned once throughout, and it is very erotic. It is a series of erotic love poems which some people think is a collection of unrelated poems and which others think were assembled to be at least somewhat cohesive.

It has always been controversial. The biggest controversy was about whether or not the Song of Songs should even be included in the Bible. Was it worthy of being "canonized" – that is, did it meet the criteria for being included in the Bible? Controversy flared in Jamnia in 90 A.D., where scholars gathered to determine once and for all the writings to be included in the Old Testament. At that time, Rabbi Akiva defended the inclusion of the Song of Songs most passionately. He said, "For all the world is not worth the day on which the Song of Songs was given to Israel, for all the writings are holy, but the Song of Songs is the Holy of Holies" (Mishnah, Yadayim 3:5).

Others were just as eloquent in saying that these erotic poems were not religious at all and certainly should not even be included in the Scriptures. But the Council of Jamnia did, in the end, include it in the Old Testament. It was considered Scripture.

The authorship of these songs is disputed. Traditionally, it was thought that King Solomon penned them. Some translations of the Bible, in fact, name the book "Song of Solomon" (NRSV). Other translations name it "Song of Songs" (NEB). Few scholars today would name Solomon as the author.

Another big issue is how to interpret these erotic love songs. The longest interpretive tradition in both Christian and Jewish circles has allegorized them, that is, to read these poems as referring to the love between God and humans. Jewish exegetes talked about the bond of mutual love between Israel and God, and Christian exegetes talked about the love bond between the Church as bride and Christ as bridegroom. These more mystical, spiritualized, or symbolic interpretations have held sway for most of the last several thousand years. Perhaps this way of reading these texts reflects some embarrassment with the quite explicitly sexual nature of these songs.

Today, this kind of allegorizing has fallen out of favour. Today, scholars (and many pastors) do a much more direct, plain sense reading (if reading poetry can ever really be a plain sense or direct reading). The "Songs" in these "Song of Songs" are simply erotic love poems between lovers. And because of this more "earthy" interpretation, preachers today are quite afraid to preach on these texts – yours truly included. When you could do an allegorical interpretation, these texts became a favourite for preachers. Many earlier preachers preached many sermons on them. Bernard of Clairvaux, in the twelfth century, preached with great frequency and eloquence on them.[1] For example:

...it is not words that are to be weighed, but feelings. Why is this so, except that holy love, which we may agree is the topic of this whole piece, is not to be valued by word or tongue, but by work and truth? Love speaks everywhere here and if anyone wishes to gain knowledge of these things which are read, they will. Otherwise, those who do not love go to hear or read a song of love in vain; since their cold breast cannot at all receive a fiery speech. For how can one who does not know Greek understand one who speaks Greek... likewise, the language of love to those who do not love will be barbarous and will be like sounding brass or tinkling cymbals (Sermon 79.1).

Today, very few sermons are preached on this book of the Bible, except perhaps at weddings, which I have done on several occasions. But this text was assigned to me. It is included in the "wisdom" literature of the Bible. And this week is "Valentine's" week. So here goes. Enjoy the poetry. Enjoy the symphony of sensuality – these songs of love.

Perhaps the story in Genesis 3 is the foil for these love songs. Genesis 3 pictures the breakdown in the relationship between Adam and Eve. It pictures their loss of intimacy. It breathes an unwelcome discordant wail of reality into the idealized Eden of Genesis 1, where Adam and Eve enjoy the garden, enjoy their relationship with God, and enjoy each other's bodies.

The tempter invites them to reach for control and for power – over the other and over the garden. Soon they are blaming each other. Soon they feel they must hide from God. Soon they sense that their feeling of intimacy is gone. They begin to feel alienated from God and from each other. And their nakedness, always something so natural, is now a source of shame. They feel they must now hide from each other and from God. Now they feel they must sew fig leaves in order to hide their genitals from each other. Genesis 3 ends with despair. These first humans hide from God because the divine-human relationship has been damaged. And they hide from each other because the male-female relationship has been damaged. The intimacy of Eden is no more.

And then along comes the Song of Songs, which revisits Eden; it revisits the way the relationship between woman and man was meant to be – and can be. It offers a new vision of healthy intimacy. The Song of Songs is a symphony of sensuality. It is poetry. It is unashamedly erotic. It is not religious in any obvious sense. God is never once mentioned in the whole book. But it seems to go back to creation, back to recover at least a glimpse of the original vision of sensuality and intimate relationships.

Three players provide all the music in this book. There are the two lovers, a woman and a man, and there are the "daughters of Jerusalem," who act as a foil and a third-party commentator to the two lovers. Sometimes, the man and woman address each other directly, and other times they speak through the daughters of Jerusalem. The poems seem to move back and forth between "distance" and "closeness," between being separated and being intimate.

It is worth noting how often the woman takes the lead in these love poems. She speaks more often than does the man. She seems to be free to make advances toward her lover. Neither the woman nor the man exploit the other. Neither dominates. Neither gender rules over the other. Here, there is a mutual exchange of love – and of bodies. Perhaps it is this total mutuality and the total absence of any kind of attempt to control the other or exert power over the other which gives beauty to this symphony. There is not even a hint of the violence of Genesis 3.

I offer a few samples of these love songs from Song of Solomon (translations from NRSV). They are not quite in a modern beat, and they have images and metaphors unfamiliar to us. The ancient readers would no doubt have been able to dance to them. You could try out some of these lines on Valentine's Day, but some of them might get you into trouble.

The woman begins the music. "For your love is better than wine, your anointing oils are fragrant, your name is perfume poured out..." (not bad!) (Song of Solomon 1:2, NRSV).

The "daughters of Jerusalem" insert an editorial comment. "We will exult and rejoice in you; we will extol your love more than wine; rightly do they love you" (1:4, NRSV).

The man responds: "I compare you, my love, to a mare among Pharaoh's chariots. Your cheeks are comely with ornaments, your neck with strings of jewels" (1:9-10, NRSV).

Woman: "My beloved is to me a bag of myrrh that lies between my breasts. My beloved is to me a cluster of henna blossoms in the vineyards of En-Gedi" (1:13-14, NRSV).

Man: "Ah, you are beautiful, my love; ah, you are beautiful; your eyes are doves. Ah, you are beautiful, my beloved, truly lovely..." (1:15-16, NRSV) — (*Is that a line that we men should memorize?*).

Woman: (Now she is at a distance, separated from her lover.) "I am a rose of Sharon, a lily of the valleys. As a lily among brambles, so is my love among maidens. With great delight, I sat in his shadow, and his fruit was sweet to my taste. He brought me to the banqueting house, and his intention toward me was love. Sustain me with raisins, refresh me with apples; for I am faint with love. O that his left hand were under my head, and that his right hand embraced me!" (2:1-6, NRSV).

There are five movements in this symphony. This first one ends, as do the others, with an intriguing comment – "I adjure you, O daughters of Jerusalem, do not stir up or awaken love until it is ready!" (2:7, NRSV). Do not stir up or awaken love until it is ready. This refrain is repeated four times. Love cannot be forced, hurried, or pressured, lest it become exploitive. Perhaps this is a healthy antidote to the exploitative pushing of sex in our society. *Do not stir up or awaken love until it is ready.*

The love poetry continues. The husband extols the bride's beauty, naming every part of her body with wondrous appreciation. "How beautiful you are, my love, how very beautiful! Your eyes are doves behind your veil. Your hair is like a flock of goats." (*I am having a hard time picturing that!*) "Your teeth are like a flock of shorn ewes that have come up from the washing... Your lips are like a crimson thread, and your mouth is lovely. Your cheeks are like halves of a pomegranate behind your veil. Your neck is like the tower of David, built in courses... Your two breasts are like two fawns, twins of a gazelle, that feed among the lilies... You are altogether beautiful, my love; there is no flaw in you..." (4:1-5,7, NRSV).

Not to be outdone, the bride crafts an eloquent poem about her lover's body. "My beloved is all radiant and ruddy, distinguished among ten thousand. His head is the finest gold; his locks are wavy, black as a raven. His eyes are like doves beside springs of water, bathed in milk, fitly set... his lips are lilies distilling liquid myrrh. His arms are rounded gold, set with jewels. His body is ivory work, encrusted with sapphire... His appearance is like Lebanon, choice as the cedars. His speech is most sweet, and he is altogether desirable..." (5:10-16, NRSV).

In the fifth and final movement, intimacy triumphs. "Set me as a seal upon your heart, as a seal upon your arm; for love is strong as death, passion fierce as the grave. Its flashes are flashes of fire, a raging flame. Many waters cannot quench love, neither can floods drown it. If one offered for love all the wealth of one's house, it would be utterly scorned" (8:6-7, NRSV).

And finally, this symphony of sensuality ends, as it must, by drawing the curtain and excluding us, the listener. The daughters of Jerusalem disappear. The listener disappears. The circle of intimacy closes on the two as they become one. "Make haste, my beloved" (8:14, NRSV).

These love poems came as a powerful alternative voice during a time when the ideals of mutuality and tender, committed love were in jeopardy. They were written in a very patriarchal world, a world that was often violent to women and saw women as the property of men. In our society too, the whole business of relationships, of sexuality, even of marriage, is desperately caught in the tension between the ideals of Genesis 1 and the violent brokenness of Genesis 3, between reflecting the image and will of God and the violence and the lust for power and control which resides deep inside each of us.

Power, domination, exploitation, control, ownership, blaming, secrecy – Or full mutuality, honesty, respect, shared passion, intimacy, and caring love. The Song of Songs plays this later music – a symphony of sensuality full of the rhythms of mutuality and respect and tenderness and intimate love.

From Genesis 3, we might despair about our sexuality, about our brokenness, about our abusive power games over another, including the one we love. The Song of Songs points us back to Genesis 1 and to the kind of sexual relationships intended by God. It points forward to a healthy, delightful intimacy with the one we love. Perhaps in spirit, it already anticipates the famous words in 1 Corinthians 13, "and the greatest of these is love."

A Little Story Challenges Abusive Power
Sermon 6: March 16, 1993

2 Samuel 11:1-5, 12: 1-9

> Have mercy on me, O God, according to your steadfast love;
> according to your abundant mercy blot out my trans-
> gressions.
>> Psalm 51:1-3, NRSV, a confession by King David

Bathsheba. There she was in the spring of the year, enjoying
the warm afternoon sun and taking a bath on the roof of her
house. There she was, naked and beautiful and, in the eyes of at
least one beholder, very sensuous. There she was, taking a bath.
Naked.

David saw her that way. King David. God's chosen King of
Israel. And he was filled with lust for her. Yes, he was already
married. And yes, Bathsheba was already married. "Who is
she?" David demands. "Bathsheba," he is told. "Bring her
to me!"

It is a demand. A king's demand. You don't ask whether

Bathsheba wants to come. This is not an invitation. It is a demand. David is king. He has complete power over her.

"Bring her to me." She is brought to David – and he rapes her.

The heading in my translation of the Bible, put there by the editors of the NRSV translation of the Bible, put there by people who should know better, reads: "David commits adultery with Bathsheba." NO! This is not adultery. Adultery is when two people with equal power decide mutually to be unfaithful to their own spouses and have sex with each other. That is sin enough. This is surely not adultery. Bathsheba has no choice in the matter. This is rape.

Whatever has happened to "good" King David?

David's Story

The story of David – King David – unfolds like a vintage success story, almost like a fairy tale story. He was the youngest, and perhaps the most inconsequential, of eight sons of Jesse, a shepherd. Young David was minding his own business and his sheep one day when the prophet Samuel visited the homestead with his anointing oil, looking for the next king of Israel. Jesse's oldest sons all filed by, each impressive in his own way, but none of them got God's signal. Finally, the text says, David came.

> Now he was ruddy, and had beautiful eyes, and was handsome... (I'm not sure why those are qualities for kingship, however) the Lord said, 'Rise and anoint him; for this is the one.' Then Samuel took the horn of oil, and anointed him in the presence of his brothers; and the Spirit of the Lord came mightily upon David from that day forward.
>
> 1 Samuel 16:10-13, NRSV

The Bible takes 42 chapters in First and Second Samuel and in First Kings to tell the many stories of David. In most of the stories, a very favourable portrait is drawn of King David. He is a hero. While still a boy soldier, David had the courage to face the fearsome giant Goliath when more seasoned soldiers trembled before him. Though David wasn't big enough or strong enough to wear a soldier's armour, David met Goliath armed only with a sling and five stones – and killed him.

David was a skilled musician. As a young lad, he plays for King Saul and soothes him enough to relieve him of his evil spirit (1 Sam 16). There are wonderful stories of David's friendship with Saul's son Jonathan. Then David marries Saul's daughter, Michal. Theirs seemed to have been a genuinely loving relationship and marriage (1 Sam 18). Eventually, King Saul feels very threatened by David's growing power and tries to kill him. There are many stories of David's daring escapes and of times when he graciously spares Saul's life (1 Sam 24, 26)

David did marry a few more wives, as kings were wont to do (1 Sam 25:39, 43). And there are many stories of successful wars and particular kindnesses. And then, suddenly, we are confronted with the story of the rape of Bathsheba. Bathsheba becomes pregnant from this rape, and the king wants to hush it all up. He brings Bathsheba's husband, Uriah, back from the battlefront, where he is one of David's best generals. "Surely," David thinks, "he will sleep with his wife, and then how is he to know that the baby isn't his?" But Uriah is a man of character and strength. He will not enjoy the comforts of home and sex while his soldiers are in deprivation and are perhaps even dying in battle.

Plan B: David tries to get Uriah drunk. Surely then he will sleep with his wife. But even that doesn't work. Finally, David orders the commander of the army to put Uriah back into battle and put him where the fighting is fiercest, and then abandon him there. The scheme works, and Uriah is killed. David has murdered him.

Problem solved. Now David can legitimately take the new widow as his wife – whether she wants to be his wife or not. Everything is covered over and handled beautifully. The secret will be kept hidden.

What about Bathsheba? Almost nothing is said of her in the Scriptures. The whole story is told from David's point of view. We are told nothing about Bathsheba's feelings, point of view, personality, or pain. I really wish we had her story, but we don't. Did she find healing? We don't know. The patriarchal culture of that time did not find it necessary that her story be told.

King David breathes a sigh of relief. He will get away with it after all. But then, a prophet shows up at his house. The prophet Nathan comes for a visit – and for some deep truth-telling. He has a story to tell. There was once a rich man and a poor man. The rich man had many sheep. The poor man had only one sheep, a family pet that was "like a daughter to him" (2 Samuel 12:3). The rich man, needing a lamb to roast for a guest, slaughters the poor man's pet sheep for the banquet.

David is outraged at hearing the story of this injustice. He can hardly wait to listen to the end of the story. He is ready to go after the rich man and kill him for this injustice.

Nathan says to David, "You are the man!" (2 Sam 12:7). You, David, king of Israel, are the rich man. You have it all. But what do you do? You steal Uriah's wife from him, you rape her, and then you have him killed. You did this evil thing, and then you tried to cover it over in deception. "For you did it secretly; but I will do this thing before all Israel, and before the sun" (2 Sam 12:12, NRSV). This is a terrible shock. The thing is exposed. It will be there for the whole nation to read – for the whole world to read. Headlines! King David has done an evil thing. He has abused his power. He raped Bathsheba and murdered Uriah, her husband.

Far beyond the *Mennonite Reporter*, this exposure. Far beyond the *Toronto Star*. It will be in the Bible, for God's sake, in the book for all the world to read for thousands of years. But what about his reputation? Yes, what about David? Shouldn't we keep his image pure? After all, he was a good king, doing so much good for his people.

And what does King David do? He confesses. He actually confesses. "I have done evil." This confession is hugely surprising – shocking even – on several levels. First, it is surprising that a prophet, with only spiritual authority, would dare confront a king. Secondly, it is surprising, even shocking, that a simple story about a poor man's lamb could break through a king's defences and layers of self-deception. And finally, shockingly, this story was recorded and put in the Bible for the whole world to read. Don't all kings deny guilt and take extreme measures not to have anything embarrassing exposed? Doesn't every community (including the church) try to hide its popular transgressors? It is astounding that this story is recorded in our Bible for posterity.

David's confession is recorded in Psalm 51, where he begins, 'Have mercy on me, O God... Wash me... Cleanse me...'

> You desire truth in the inward being; therefore teach me wisdom in my secret heart. Purge me with hyssop, and I shall be clean; wash me, and I shall be whiter than snow. Let me hear joy and gladness; let the bones that you have crushed rejoice. Hide your face from my sins, and blot out all my iniquities. Psalm 51:6-9, NRSV

This powerful Psalm is much read and much loved. It speaks a deep truth to all of us. Many composers have set it to music. It resonates deep within our souls. At some level, we can all identify with David's plea for mercy and for cleansing and for forgiveness. We all have confessions to make.

Shockingly — a prophet with no legal standing and only moral and spiritual authority dares to confront a king; instead of silencing the prophet, the king repents; and this story of sin and repentance is recorded in the Bible for the whole world to read.

This story is a very hopeful one. It tells us that all of us, from the most powerful people on earth to those of us who feel small and powerless, sometimes abuse other people. The good news is that all of us can repent and receive forgiveness – when there is genuine repentance.

And yet, this story ends on a very sad note. Says the text, "The Lord struck the child that Uriah's wife bore to David, and it became very ill... on the seventh day the child died" (2 Sam 12:15-18, NRSV).

An important caveat: We can look to God for forgiveness. But let's not expect or demand forgiveness from those we have deeply wounded. We cannot press the Bathshebas of this world for quick forgiveness. Pressing them may further wound them.

Afterword

I tell this story as a part of our Lenten series, "Restore to us the joy of salvation." I am convinced that "confession" is a big part of restoring our joy. It may be that it is in confession and repentance that we will find a new delight in our walk with God.

Confession: Acknowledging how we have failed, how we continue to miss God's mark for us. Acknowledging how we have hurt others, how we have broken relationships, how we live with brokenness and alienation and guilt. If we have wounded others sexually, we have very particular confessions to make.

Repentance: Repentance is so much more than only feeling sorry for what we have done. Rather, it is changing what we do now so that we can heal our relationships, heal our brokenness, and heal our spirit.

We long for forgiveness – forgiveness for the pain we have caused others and ourselves. We long to restore our broken relationships.

> *Have mercy on me, O God,*
>   *according to your steadfast love...*
>   *Create in me a clean heart, O God...*
>   *Restore to me the joy of your salvation.*

Esther: the Sexy, Violent Book?
Sermon 7: January 24, 1988

What is the Book of Esther doing in the Bible?

I made the mistake this week of reading the book of Esther in the Bible. You see, this is the last Sunday before Valentine's Day, and I wanted to pick out a love story in the Bible and use it to talk about romance and other pleasant things appropriate to this season of the year. Beats thinking about our severe winter weather. At other times around Valentine's Day, I have preached about the Song of Songs, about Hosea and Gomer, and about Samson and Delilah. These last two are very difficult love stories to preach about. Maybe it is very foolish to add to that list the story of Esther and King Xerxes.

But I read the Book of Esther and got hooked. And that really was a mistake because this story has little to do with romance. The relationship between Esther and King Xerxes is not a model to idealize. God is not once mentioned. The whole book has no direct religious quality to it. The closest the story comes to any religious overtones at all is the statement by Mordecai to Esther, "Who knows? Perhaps you have come to royal dignity for just such a time as this" (Esther 4:14, NRSV). This statement just barely hints at some bigger purpose in everything that is happening.

But, as I said, I got hooked on the story. It has all the ingredients of a great drama. If it were made into a movie, it might well beat out "Amadeus" for the Academy Awards. The story of Esther is filled with court intrigue, violence, sex, good guys and bad guys, and a massacre. What more could you want in a movie? And, of course, the beautiful but poor Jewish girl marries the most powerful king in the world. She then risks her life to save her people. Ever since, the Jewish people have celebrated that event with the "Feast of Purim."

But is this story worth preaching about? Should it even have been included in our Bible? It does not seem to have many applications to our lives – at least not direct applications. And still, shouldn't the whole Bible be grist for the preacher's mill?

So here goes. I will warn you ahead of time that my conclusion may seem weak to some.

Time – Not long after the end of the Babylonian exile, probably around 480 B.C.E.

Place – Susa, the capital city of ancient Persia. By the time of this story, the Persians had taken over from the Babylonians as rulers of the ancient world. Many of the Israelite exiles had returned home to Jerusalem, but there were still many exiles scattered throughout the Persian empire and quite a few, apparently, in Susa, the capital city.

Cast of Characters

The King. The name given to him in some translations of the Bible is Ahasuerus. The abbreviated form is Xerxes, and that is the name history knows. Xerxes was an absolute monarch. His every whim was obeyed. He surrounded his court with wine, women, and wealth. To him, life was cheap.

Vashti. She was the queen, the only legitimate wife of the king. It is thought that she was the daughter of King Nebuchadnezzar. Vashti is only a minor character in this drama. She apparently has too much spunk for the king to tolerate. The king demands that she come to him. She refused. He became enraged. "For this deed of the queen will be made known to all women, causing them to look with contempt on their husbands" (Esther 1:17, NRSV). She is summarily dismissed. The king adds, "every man should be master in his own house" (Esther 1:22, NRSV). The king needs a new consort. Esther enters the story.

Esther. She is an orphan girl. She is the adopted daughter of Mordecai. She is described as being "fair and beautiful" (2:7). She was so beautiful and lovely that she caught the King's eye.

Mordecai. He was a Jewish captive, brought against his will to Susa. He probably held a very minor position in the palace, perhaps being the porter at the gate. That did give him access to the palace, so he knew what was going on there. He was a cousin to Esther and her adoptive father.

Haman. He is the villain in the story — power-hungry, greedy, and wealthy. He plotted skillfully against anyone who might be a threat to him, and he had a hatred for Jews. He was next to the king in power.

The Plot – Scene 1

King Xerxes throws a big feast – a six-month-long big feast. Six months gives time for all the foreign dignitaries to arrive. During one of these feast days, he drinks a bit too much wine.

He orders his wife, Queen Vashti, to appear before him in order to display her beauty to the people and the officers, "for she was fair to behold," says the account (1:11). But it was not custom, or decent, for an oriental king's wife to appear before strange men. So, Vashti refuses. The situation becomes delicate. On the one hand, she has the right to refuse the request. On the other hand, the king has absolute power. The angry king summons his lawyers to see what he can do to punish his disobedient wife.

Their advice? Queen Vashti has done wrong, and not to the king alone, but also to all the officers and to all the peoples in all the provinces. Why, every woman will come to know what the queen has done, and this will make them treat their husbands with contempt; they will say, King Xerxes ordered Queen Vashti to be brought before him, and she did not come. The great ladies of Persia and Median, who have heard of the queen's conduct, will tell all the king's officers of this day, and there will be endless disrespect and insolence (1:16-18).

Nip this woman's liberation thing in the bud immediately, or else we won't be able to control our wives either. Make a royal decree. Write a new law of the Persians and the Medes that Vashti is banished forever from your sight. Send this decree throughout the land, "declaring that every man should be master in his own house" (Esther 1:22, NRSV).

Poor Queen Vashti is written out of the story.

New Queen – Scene 2

The king is without a wife, poor fellow, and the land without a queen. That would never do. So, after his temper tantrum subsides, Xerxes orders his commissioners to seek out all the beautiful young virgins in the land so that he can choose the one that pleases him the most. One of these, a stunning beauty, is the one that pleases him the most – yes, the poor Jewish girl Esther. She does not let on that she is Jewish. Subject people are not looked on with great favour. Play that part down.

When it is finally Esther's time to please the king (sexually?), she does, and he is completely charmed and smitten. The account says, "the king loved Esther more than all the other women; of all the virgins she won his favor and devotion, so that he set the royal crown on her head and made her queen instead of Vashti. Then the king gave a great banquet to all his officials and ministers—"Esther's banquet." He also granted a holiday to the provinces, and gave gifts with royal liberality" (Esther 2:17-18, NRSV).

The Plot – Scene 3

Now we begin to get into the heavy intrigue stuff. Several disaffected members of the king's court plot to kill the king. Mordecai, the Jew, happens to overhear the plot and reveals it to the king. The two rebellious chaps are hanged, and Mordecai's good deed is written into the royal chronicle in the presence of the king. This will become very important as the story unfolds.

Enter Haman, the villain of the story. Haman is second in importance only to the king. When Haman entered a room, everyone bowed to him and did obeisance. Except for Mordecai, that is. Stubborn Jew that he was, he would bow down only to the Lord God, not to another man. But that infuriated Haman and he plotted revenge. He looked to lay hands on him alone and looked for a way to destroy all the Jews throughout the whole kingdom, Mordecai and all his race (3:6).

Haman plotted his evil revenge. First, he cast lots, called "Pur" in Persian, to find the best day for the massacre. He tells the king, "There is a certain people scattered and separated among the peoples in all the provinces of your kingdom; their laws are different from those of every other people, and they do not keep the king's laws, so that it is not appropriate for the king to tolerate them. If it pleases the king, let a decree be issued for their destruction, and I will pay ten thousand talents of silver into the hands of those who have charge of the king's business, so that they may put it into the king's treasuries" (Esther 3:8-9, NRSV).

This sounds very reasonable – and profitable – to the king. He signs the decree and sends orders to all the provinces "to destroy, to kill, and to annihilate all Jews, young and old, women and children, in one day, the thirteenth day of the twelfth month, the month of Adar, and to plunder their goods" (Esther 3:13, NRSV).

Counter Plot – Scene 4

Mordecai and Esther confer together after this terrible decree is issued. Mordecai feels that it may be "just for a time such as this" that Esther has been chosen to be queen. There may just be a larger purpose – a God-ordained purpose – for Esther to be queen now during this awful crisis. Esther must go to the king. This will be both dangerous – and against the law. No one goes to the king, not even the queen. The king calls whom he wants to see – and whom he wants to have sex with. He might kill anyone who comes to him unbidden.

Esther says to Mordecai, "Go, gather all the Jews to be found in Susa, and hold a fast on my behalf; and neither eat nor drink for three days, night or day. I and my maids will also fast as you do." (Is this a hint of at least some religious concern?) "After that I will go to the king, though it is against the law; and if I perish, I perish" (Esther 4:16-17, NRSV).

But Esther is not only courageous – she is also very crafty. She wins the king's favour (we can imagine with sexual seduction) but tells him nothing of her larger scheming. She beats around the bush a lot. Then, she invites the king to a banquet and invites Haman as well. The first banquet is just for good times and to soften up the king. But here she baits her trap. Meanwhile, Haman again meets Mordecai, who still refuses to bow down to him. Haman, in rage, orders a 75-foot-high gallows to be built for Mordecai's hanging.

In terrific spirits, Haman goes to the second banquet planned by Esther. Life couldn't be better, visions of Mordecai swinging on the gallows filling him with delight.

Meanwhile, King Xerxes has had a sleepless night, and instead of counting sheep, he reads the royal chronicles of daily events and is reminded that Mordecai saved his life a while ago and hasn't yet been rewarded for it. When Haman comes in, the king asks him what an appropriate reward would be for someone he favours. Haman assumes that it is himself who is to be honoured. He waxes eloquent about what would be an appropriate reward – royal robes, royal crown, royal horse, and a royal parade through the city.

"Excellent," says Xerxes. "Let's do all that for Mordecai." Haman, who was just about to request permission to hang Mordecai, sulks off to the banquet. There, the trap closes. The king, over wine, says to Queen Esther, "What is your request? It shall be given you, even to the half of my kingdom, it shall be fulfilled" (Esther 5:3, NRSV).

Till now, Esther has not yet let on to the King that she is a Jew. But this is the opening she needs. "If I have found favour with your majesty, and if it please your majesty, my request and petition is that my own life and the lives of my people may be spared. For we have been sold, I and my people, to be destroyed, slain, and exterminated" (Esther 7:3-4, NRSV).

The king explodes, asking, who has done this awful thing? An adversary and an enemy, said Esther, "this wicked Haman"

(7:6). (Esther does not mention that it was the king himself who actually signed the orders.) Poor Haman. He is hanged on the gallows he had erected for Mordecai.

Scene 5: What about the Old Law?

The "enemy" was dead. But there was still a problem. A law written in the king's name and sealed with the king's seal cannot be revoked. Thus says "the law of the Medes and the Persians." The order to kill all the Jews stands. The king is helpless before Esther's pleading.

Ah, but a second decree might be in order. "The king allowed the Jews who were in every city to assemble and defend their lives, to destroy, to kill, and to annihilate any armed force of any people or province that might attack them" (Esther 8:11, NRSV).

The Jews fasted and holidayed and gained many converts. "On the very day when the enemies of the Jews hoped to gain power over them, but which had been changed to a day when the Jews would gain power over their foes, the Jews gathered in their cities throughout all the provinces of King Xerxes to lay hands on those who sought their ruin; and no one could withstand them, because the fear of them had fallen upon all peoples" (Esther 9:1-2, NRSV).

Post-Script

The Jewish people have ever since celebrated this victory with the Feast of Purim. Remember that "Pur" is the Persian word for the casting of the lot. The day that was intended for their destruction became the day of their salvation.

As for Mordecai? He became second in power only to Xerxes. He was a great man among the Jews and was popular with the mass of his countrymen, for he sought the good of his people and promoted the welfare of all their descendants (10:3).

As for Queen Esther? "The command of Queen Esther fixed these practices of Purim, and it was recorded in writing" (Esther 9:32, NRSV).

Afterword

Question – Why is the book of Esther even in the Bible? Is it appropriate to tell this story of sexual games and violence in church? Or in Sunday School? There is very little that is religious in it. It is for this reason, in fact, that it took far longer than normal for Esther to be accepted into the Hebrew canon of Scripture. But eventually, it became part of our Bible. Why did it take so long, and why was it finally included? It makes some sense that the Jewish people, who celebrate the feast of Purim which grew out of this story, would see it as Scripture. Is it a story that Christians too can claim?

It is a captivating story. It is a terrific read. It does deal with sexual violence and abuse. It does hold Haman accountable for his abuse. It does not hold King Xerxes accountable. And Esther? She basically exploits her sexual allure in the long game of freeing her own people. And succeeds. Maybe we need to take more account of the minor characters such as Vashti, whose courage and wisdom are not explored in detail in the Bible, for some direction for our own lives.

It reminds me that dealing with sexual violence is complicated. We struggle in the church to deal responsibly with it. The book of Esther is one more piece in the longer story of violence, racism, and abusive sex. Does it answer all our contemporary questions? Probably not. But it is a terrific read, even while we ponder its relevance for today.

Love, Adultery, and Love Again

Sermon 8: February 12, 1989

Hosea 11

Valentine's Day always was a lot of fun – except perhaps for the Charlie Browns of this world who just keep on waiting for that card which never comes while all around them, other children are getting cards by the dozen. There is romance in the air: sweet, mushy, sloppy, sentimental, idealized romance. We could do with a dose of that about now, couldn't we?

So why then preach on the story of Hosea and Gomer, where all romantic illusions are destroyed? Why? Because love is so much deeper than only romance, and because the story of Hosea and Gomer rewrites the definition of love.

Today is not only Valentine's Day – it is also the first Sunday of Lent – a time to begin focusing on the story of Jesus, the one who loved us so much that he died for us. Hosea's kind of love begins to help us understand God's kind of love. There is a parallel between Hosea's story and Jesus' story.

I am, of course, all for romance and for Valentine's-day and for "guess who's coming to dinner" (a long TUMC tradition of organizing a lunch where hosts and guests meet as a surprise to both). There is just a touch of the incurable romance in my soul, though domestically, for a man who makes his living with words, I am too stingy with the romantic ones – I confess.

The Story of Hosea and Gomer

This is a love story. But it is a very disturbing love story – profoundly disturbing. Upon reading it, the story sounds almost surreal, improbable or impossible. It is a wrenching drama, graphic, x-rated, but decidedly not pornographic. Its explicitness makes a powerful statement about the depth of love which we can hardly fathom.

We set the stage for this drama. Hosea has been called by God to an almost impossible task. He is to be God's prophet, God's spokesperson, at a time when Israel has no ears at all for God. Israel's days are numbered already in that time, just before 722 B.C. World super-power Assyria is flexing its expansionist muscles. It will soon impose its will on everyone. In the face of the inevitable, little Israel and little Syria try to play the political game. They cleverly forge alliances and make treaties. They devise strategies. It is all a desperate ploy to save themselves from being obliterated by Assyria.

It won't work, thunders Hosea. It can't work. You are ignoring the real problem. The root problem is not the Assyrians at all. Look within yourself, not at the outside. The rot is within. Instead of making treaties and strategizing, clean up the internal mess. It is not that the Lord has abandoned you but that you have abandoned the Lord.

It is the most idolatrous period of Israel's history. Baalism is at its height, fully re-introduced again 200 years after Elijah rooted it out. Central to Baal worship were the fertility cults, including sacred prostitution, a way to symbolize and re-enact the fertility rights.

And suddenly, the image clicks for Hosea. Israel is being unfaithful. Israel is like an unfaithful spouse who takes in other lovers. She has taken as a new lover, the god Baal, while still pretending to be in marriage with Yahweh God. This marriage is broken. It is a sham. The love relationship is destroyed. The marriage has disintegrated.

Marriage is a covenant. Yahweh God and the people of Israel had made a covenant with each other – a covenant to be faithful to each other.

> Then God spoke all these words: I am the Lord your God, who brought you out of the land of Egypt, out of the house of slavery; you shall have no other gods before me.
> Exodus 20:1-3, NRSV

What happens when one party breaks the covenant, is unfaithful, and takes in other lovers? How long will God endure the numerous affairs of the promiscuous spouse, asks Hosea? Shouldn't there be a swift divorce and be done with it? The covenant is broken, the relationship fractured – love is dead. Hosea pictures a divine sadness, a pathos. Says Yahweh God:

> When Israel was a child, I loved him, and out of Egypt
> I called my son. The more I called them, the more they
> went from me; they kept sacrificing to the Baals, and
> offering incense to idols. Yet it was I who taught
> Ephraim to walk, I took them up in my arms; but they
> did not know that I healed them. I led them with cords
> of human kindness, with bands of love.
> Hosea 11:1-4, NRSV

But God will not divorce God's unfaithful bride. There is, instead, an incredible invitation to renew the covenant.

> My heart recoils within me; my compassion grows
> warm and tender. I will not execute my fierce anger; I
> will not again destroy Ephraim; for I am God and no
> mortal, the Holy One in your midst, and I will not
> come in wrath.
> Hosea 11:8-9, NRSV

Hosea's Personal Story

Hosea's personal story begins to mirror the national story. It becomes a sordid soap opera-like ordeal. He marries Gomer, a woman who has most likely submitted herself to the Canaanite bridal rites of initiation. That is, she is one of the temple prostitutes.

"When the Lord first spoke through Hosea, the Lord said to Hosea, 'Go, take for yourself a wife of whoredom and have children of whoredom, for the land commits great whoredom by forsaking the Lord.' So he went and took Gomer daughter of Diblaim, and she conceived and bore him a son" (Hosea 1:2-3, NRSV).

Hosea and Gomer have three children: a son, a daughter, and another son. They each are given names with a particular meaning. It is as if the children of the prophet are going to be "walking billboards." By the third child, some things are becoming clear, and Hosea calls him "Lo-ammi," which means "not my son." Who knows who the father is?

Things go from bad to worse domestically. Gomer finally gives up even the pretense of a marriage relationship, leaves Hosea, and openly lives out the life of a temple prostitute – which everyone knows her to be anyway. But even that has a worst-case scenario. She becomes enslaved by a pimp. He uses her until the inevitable aging makes her unattractive. And when she has no more sexual value, he puts this used-up, worthless prostitute's body on the slave auction market block. Perhaps someone will pay a few shekels so that she can perform other kinds of slave labour.

And who should be there at the auction mart ready to buy this useless, discarded woman? Her husband is there. Somehow, he has kept in touch. Somehow, he has heard of the wares being auctioned off. And after all those hellish, degrading years, Hosea is there in the front row of that ring where everyone can see him, raising his arms and shouting that he will outbid everyone to buy her back.

"Sold," yells the auctioneer. "Sold to Hosea, Prophet of the most-high God, sold one very sorry-looking and used-up prostitute." He makes out the bill of sale.

"I got her back for fifteen pieces of silver, a homer of barley, and a measure of wine," says Hosea in a matter-of-fact way. "She is my wife."

Turning to his bought-back wife, Hosea says simply, Gomer, many a long day you shall live in my house and not be adulterous anymore. We are husband and wife again.

A love-story? Yes. But not a pretty story. A gut-wrenching love story.

The Universal Story

Suddenly, the parallels become clear. Hosea's personal story has become a mirror of the divine story, his pathos a picture of the divine pathos. This is also the story of God and God's people. A covenant was made, like a marriage covenant, and then broken. God's people were unfaithful, prostituting themselves with other gods. Now, surely, God will write a bill of divorce and be done with this sordid affair.

Shockingly, we hear the Lord say, How can I give you up? How can I hand you over?... My heart is changed within me. All my compassion is aroused... For I am God and not human. Come back to me.

And suddenly, another flash of insight sears its way into our own hearts, at first repulsive and then gradually exhilarating. We ourselves are Gomer. That is the character in the story we have to identify with. We are often unfaithful to God. We prostitute ourselves to other values, other gods, and other priorities. We break the covenant and go our own way. We get sucked up into the various cultic manifestations of our day.

And if we are Gomer, isn't it good to know that God continues to love us? God is there at the slave market, personally intervening, raising arms and shouting to outbid everyone else for us. We are invited back regardless of our sordid story. God says to us through Hosea, "Return, O Israel, to the Lord your God; for you have stumbled... Return to the Lord" (Hos 14:1-2, NRSV).

"And I will take you for my wife forever; I will take you for my wife in righteousness and in justice, in steadfast love, and in mercy. I will take you for my wife in faithfulness; and you shall know the Lord"(Hos 2:19, NRSV).

Then the Lord vows,
I will show my love to the one I called 'Not my loved one.'
I will say to those called 'Not my people,' 'You are my people';
and they will say, 'You are my God.' (Hos 2:23, NIV)

The Jesus Story

God will demonstrate his love in another way. God will send the Son – Jesus – as an invitation to us to enter the covenant. Jesus will enter our very human world. He will live, teach, and model God's love. Jesus will be the divine love story. That kind of love is beyond our comprehension. It is beyond our capacity. We humans will turn away from him. Better that this Jesus die rather than that we humans be confronted daily by the love of God extended to enemies and to Gomers and to all of us – whether we are faithful or not. We humans thought that when we drove Jesus to the cross, God's love would be extinguished, taken back. But even from the cross – and from the auction marts of this world – God's hands remain open, inviting, and forgiving.

Hosea goes to the auction block and buys his unfaithful wife, Gomer, back. And continues to love her.

During this time of Lent, we are invited to re-enter the Jesus story. It is a love story, an incredible, incomprehensible, divine love story. Whether we have been faithful or unfaithful, God's love surrounds us and welcomes us into God's covenant.

"Sold," yells the auctioneer. *"Sold to God."*

Sex, Intimacy & Violence – the Story of Samson
Sermon 9: February 18, 2007

Judges 13-16

"Please be my valentine. Come, cupid, shoot your arrows into our hearts, make us fall madly in love, instantly, magically." Valentine's Day has slipped by us once again. Was yours a hugely romantic day? Or were you disappointed that your "love" was not returned? In keeping with the season, let's find a good love story, maybe a love story out of the Bible. Will the story of Samson and Delilah do? But then, we may ask, why is this story even in the Bible? It is a love story, all right, but one that ends in tragedy. It is a love story gone bad.

Maclean's magazine devotes two recent issues to love gone bad. Its January 29 issue highlights an article entitled "The 27-year itch." More and more of us older couples are calling it quits after decades of marriage. Apparently, we older couples are finding it more and more difficult to stay in love with each other. The statistics are quite appalling. And then, *Maclean's* February 19 issue focuses on the other end of the age spectrum and tells us that teenagers and young people are either refusing to fall in love or can't fall in love. They have sex a lot, but this sex is never connected with love or commitment. The authors use the phrase "hooking up," which apparently means pursuing sex but delaying love and resisting committed relationships. Love can wait. Sex can't. Multiple sexual partners are the norm, they say. But the end of this loveless sex, according to many interviews with these same teens, is emptiness and meaninglessness and loneliness – *because there is never any genuine intimacy.*

Intimacy – The Fragile Miracle

Intimacy is, at heart, a sense of closeness with another or closeness with a group. Or closeness with God. And that closeness with another has more to do with a sharing of feelings, ideas, concerns, or experiences, than it does with a sharing of bodies. At its best, sexual intercourse is an expression of intimacy. At its worst, it is an escape from real intimacy.

Intimacy is an emotional closeness, a meeting of meanings, a communion between persons. It is those moments when two persons – or a group of people – make deep contact with each other. It is an emotional and personal communion, a deep sharing of thoughts, ideas, and feelings – moments when people look eye to eye into each other's very being. Intimacy is a bridge connecting one person with the core of being of another person, and over which there is a mutual flow of feelings, hopes, anxieties, dreams, and sometimes the physical expression of love.

But intimacy is never a permanent thing. It is not something that you achieve and then have forever. It is not something that is there every minute of a marriage or of any relationship. We long for genuine intimacy, and yet it is often elusive. It wants to slip through our fingers, and loneliness is never far away. It remains almost a mystery. But when we experience it, it is a very beautiful mystery indeed.

I want to suggest that there are two poles to an intimate relationship – both closeness and distance, both togetherness and apartness, both inviting the other to be near and allowing the other space. There needs to be a rhythm in the relationship, an ebb and flow between the two poles – between touching and letting go.

Anne Morrow Lindbergh, in her book *Gift From The Sea*, writes poetically about the two poles of intimacy.[1] She likens the patterns of touch in a good relationship to those of a dance in which heavy, possessive clutching or even clinging are not acceptable. Rather, the dance unfolds with "endlessly changing beauty." There may instead be the "barest touch in passing," but the partners move in the same rhythm, and are "nourished by it."

If we strive too frantically for closeness, if we become possessive of another, if we always want to be near, the relationship will begin to feel suffocating, stifling, and very un-free. We want to pull away from the clinging vine, but if there is too much apart-ness, if space is the norm and distance predominates, intimacy does not happen either. In a healthy relationship, intimacy moves in the rhythm between the two poles of closeness and apart-ness — of drawing near and letting go.

For all that is said of intimacy, and it may already be an overused cliché, in the end, it is still a gift, a happening, a miracle. You cannot force it to happen, but you can open yourself to allowing it to happen. And when you have a relationship that offers intimacy, accept it as a gift from God, rejoice and know that you are richly blessed.

Intimacy as a Game – the Story of Samson

For many people, intimacy is only a game. So it was for Samson and his various lovers. In Judges 13-16 is an intriguing set of stories. The theme is intimacy, but it is intimacy as a game, and the game ends in tragedy, as all of that kind of game-playing must.

When I re-read these stories, I wondered why they were even in the Bible. There is no model here for how we should live or how we should love. Why all this space in the Bible for a very unappealing character? More puzzling yet is why we find Samson's name in the book of Hebrews in the New Testament. There, in chapter 11, he is included in the list of the heroes of faith, his name included among the saints. Well, maybe if sinners like Samson make it onto that list, there is hope for us all. I do admit that there is something very appealing about stories of people who are super-humanly strong. Headlines: "Strongest man in the world runs amuck and kills 1,000 people with the jawbone of a donkey." That would make the 6:00 news. Might even get him his own TV series.

His story does begin with a lot of promise. His birth is announced by an angel. His mother is barren, so her pregnancy must have required divine intervention. His mother was told that this baby was to be dedicated to the Lord in a Nazarite vow, that is, specifically consecrated to God for a special purpose. There were three parts to the Nazarite vow.

1. The person must abstain from drinking any alcoholic beverages.
2. The person must avoid any contact with a dead body, human or animal.
3. The person must never have his or her hair cut.

In these stories about Samson, it is clear that he will violate each of these vows. We turn to his birth story. The angel who announces his birth lays a huge assignment on him. He is to begin the deliverance of Israel from the hands of the Philistines. A close reading of this story suggests a problem. The Nazarite vow was supposed to be a personal vow made with full awareness of all the implications, which would assume it was made by an adult who had such awareness. In this story, it is Samson's mother who makes the vow on Samson's behalf. The mother so wanted her son to do the right thing. Samson does not make that vow himself, and it seems that he never really does accept his call from God. He is always fighting against it. (He seems, in fact, to be always fighting.)

His story is going to be one grand drama after another. I want to focus on only two shorter segments of the overall story. I doubt whether these are the places the original tellers and editors of the story would have focused on. For today, I am not really interested in Samson's superhuman feats of strength, as good a read as they are. Instead, I want to focus on his love life – the heart of his relationships with the two primary women in his life. Well, three, actually. In those relationships, many words of intimacy are exchanged, but there is no experience of real intimacy. In that, there is a powerful message for us in our day.

Marriage

In episode one, Samson sets out to get married.

> Once Samson went down to Timnah, and at Timnah he saw a Philistine woman. Then he came up, and told his father and mother, 'I saw a Philistine woman at Timnah; now get her for me as my wife.' But his father and mother said to

him, 'Is there not a woman among your kin, or among all our people, that you must go to take a wife from the uncircumcised Philistines?' But Samson said to his father, 'Get her for me, because she pleases me.' Judges 14:1-4, NRSV

Seems rather impulsive. Doesn't sound like he discussed the thing with the girl or with her parents. "I like her. Get her for me." It does make courtship easier if you can do that. His parents don't like this idea at all. She is, after all, a foreigner, an "enemy," and one of a different faith. None of this makes any difference to Samson.

Samson sets out to visit this woman and on the way encounters a lion. The text tells the story, how the spirit of the Lord came on him with power, so that he tore the lion apart with his bare hands (Judges 14:6). This is the first time in his story that there is a hint of his extraordinary strength. His great strength seems to be connected with the spirit of the Lord "compelling" him. It is connected with his Nazarite vow.

This dead lion will play a part in his wedding story. His parents have arranged the wedding, and on their way to the bride's home, Samson and his parents come across the lion he killed earlier. They notice a swarm of bees making honey in that carcass. Samson takes the honey from the carcass – thereby violating the vow not to touch a dead body – and eats it. Then Samson uses this experience to craft a riddle. During the seven-day wedding celebration, Samson wants to have some "fun." He makes a huge bet with 30 of his new wife's friends (thirty linen garments and thirty sets of clothes). They must guess his riddle. "Out of the eater came something to eat. Out of the strong came something sweet" (Judges 14:14, NRSV). He is referring, of course, to the honey from the lion. They can't figure it out, so they pressure his wife to get the answer from Samson.

She throws herself on him, sobbing, You only hate me, you don't love me, you have put a riddle to my countrymen, and you have not told me what it is. When you love each other, you don't keep secrets, my dear. Come on, share with your dear wife (Judges 13:16). Words of intimacy. But the sharing of secrets is for an ulterior motive. It is to tell her countrymen the answer to the riddle so that they will win the bet.

The secret is told. Samson is betrayed. He has lost his bet and must pay up. He flies into a rage. He stages a magnificent temper tantrum, leaves his wife, and kills a bunch of Philistines. In the best of soap opera traditions, his wife goes over to the best man at the wedding and sleeps with him. When Samson hears about this, he kills a bunch more of the Philistines and burns their crops as well by catching a number of jackals (foxes), tying them together by their tails, two by two, and adding a torch.

In the ongoing story of Samson, there is an ongoing escalation of the cycle of violence and abuse. Next comes a short episode of Samson hiring a prostitute, buying love, as it were. If he couldn't relate to women, he could still buy sex, we are told.

Samson and Delilah

Delilah enters the story. Enter real love, or at least what seems to be love, especially in contrast to the prostitutes he has been seeing. Has Samson learned anything at all?

Samson and Delilah. Sweet love at last. But Samson's new love is not above betrayal either. The Philistines bribe Delilah to find out the secrets of Samson's strength (1,100 shekels of silver from each of the lords). Wouldn't it be tempting to betray even the one you love for instant riches? Delilah and Samson play games with each other – power games. Tell me the secrets of your heart, Samson dearest. Tell me the source of your strength (Judges 16:6). Of course, my love. Would I hold anything from you? My strength lives in my being free. If anyone ties me up, why I'll be just like an ordinary man (Judges 16:7). The game goes on for quite a while. After each instalment, quite a few Philistines lose their lives. Finally, Delilah, in a profession of deep love, says:

> How can you say, I love you, when your heart is not
> with me? You have mocked me these three times, and
> you have not told me where in your great strength lies.
> And she pressed him hard with her words, day after
> day, and urged him until his soul was vexed to death.
> And he told her all his mind. Judges 16:15, NRSV

Delilah demands intimacy. Come dear, tell me the secrets of your heart. When you are in love, you share everything. There shouldn't be any secrets between us, dear. And finally, Samson does share his deepest secret – his vow with God, the core of his identity. And he is immediately betrayed. Delilah first makes love to him, and then, when he falls asleep, cuts off his hair. The final Nazarite vow is broken. His strength leaves him. The Philistines capture him, gouge out his eyes, and force him to grind flour at the mill. He is now their slave.

Words of intimacy. From both Delilah and Samson. But not real intimacy. The words have an ulterior purpose.

The story will end with revenge. Samson never did live out of obedience to his call from God. He always acted out of ever deeper levels of rage and revenge. Now, his hair grows back. He is still a slave. His enemies take him to a temple gathering honouring their god, Dagon. He is brought there to be mocked. Now, with his strength restored, in one final act of revenge, he pulls down the pillars of the temple, killing everyone inside – including himself. Samson does not fulfill his destiny or follow his calling. There is no lasting peace brought about with the Philistines, although he has killed many.

Intimacy and Violence

Our world cries out for intimacy. We all long for intimate relationships – the depth sharing, person to person, that touches the innermost depth of our very being with loving, healing encounters. But the word itself seems almost to have lost its potency, its power, its promise of reaching our deepest needs. Our overly sexualized world associates intimacy mostly with sex, and not necessarily with loving sex. And when sex isn't loving, we are close to entering the world of abuse and violence.

Intimacy – an emotional and spiritual closeness with another – or with a group. Genuine intimacy takes time, and effort, to develop, whether that intimacy is with God, with another person, or with a group of people. Samson and Delilah shared many beautiful, intimate words with each other. But they used them violently and abusively. That is a warning for our world where even in our churches, we hear the stories of people in power using intimate words but violating people.

Afterword

Intimacy is a beautiful word. Intimacy is a beautiful thing. But intimacy is fragile – I call it a fragile miracle. It happens when we open ourselves deeply – to God, to another, to a community. You can't achieve intimacy with a power move. You can only reach an intimate relationship by making yourself vulnerable and by opening your heart to one you have learned to trust. Receive intimacy then as a gift, even a miracle, fragile but precious, free of even any hints of coercion or violence. Can the story of Samson teach us that?

Racism, Love and Sex – the Story of Ruth
Sermon 10: date unknown

Ruth 1-4, Deuteronomy 24:19-22

The context for understanding the radicalness of the story of Ruth is the deep racism expressed by the prophet Ezra. The remnants of the exile to Babylon have just returned home to Jerusalem – and to chaos. Ezra feels called by God to denounce the mixed marriages which were happening when returning exiles met those who now inhabited Jerusalem.

> For they [returning exile men] have taken some of their daughters [daughters of these foreigners now living in Jerusalem], as wives for themselves and for their sons. Thus the holy seed has mixed itself with the peoples of the lands, and in this faithlessness the officials and leaders have led the way. Ezra 9:2, NRSV

Ezra demands an end to these marriages. There follows the heart-rending account of families torn apart when Jewish men were required to get rid of their foreign wives.

In our story today, in a time of famine, Naomi and Abimelech flee to Moab for survival. They have two sons, Mahlon and Chilion. Both marry Moabite wives (really, there was no other choice open to them – there would have been no Jewish women available). The story becomes tragic. All three of the men die, leaving Naomi and her two daughters-in-law, Orpah and Ruth, as widows – and destitute.

What now? Naomi has been reduced to bitterness and enormous guilt. Is God punishing her for allowing her sons to marry Moabites? She laments, back then, my stomach was empty, but my heart and womb were full. Now my stomach is full, and my heart and womb are empty (Ruth 1:21).

Naomi decides to go back to Jerusalem. She urges Orpah and Ruth to leave her and return to their people. Orpah does. Ruth insists she will stay with Naomi. The scene is set for the next phase of this marvellous story, set now in Jerusalem.

Naomi will finally return home to Jerusalem. She is ready to face the taunting "I told you so's" that she will face. She will face the censure of her people and return husbandless, child-less, heirless, empty, and bitter. She couldn't have imagined what Ruth will bring to her story. It is Ruth who makes a pledge to Naomi:

> Where you go, I will go; where you lodge, I will lodge, your people shall be my people, and your God my God. Where you die, I will die – there will I be buried. May the Lord do thus and so to me, and more as well, if even death parts me from you! (Ruth 1:16-17, NRSV).

But how will Naomi and Ruth survive in Bethlehem, impoverished and scandalized as they are? We are let in on a rather fortunate circumstance. "Now Naomi had a kinsman on her husband's side, a prominent rich man, of the family of Elimelech, whose name was Boaz" (Ruth 2:1, NRSV).

It is the time of the barley harvest, and Ruth goes out behind the reapers to glean left-over ears of barley. Gleaning was an honourable way for the poor to get food. It was socially acceptable assistance that maintained respect and dignity for the poor. Moses had insisted on it, he decreed,

> When you reap your harvest in your field and forget a sheaf in the field, you shall not go back to get it; it shall be left for the alien, the orphan, and the widow, so that the Lord your God may bless you in all your undertakings. When you beat your olive trees, do not strip what is left; it shall be for the alien, the orphan, and the widow. When you gather the grapes of your vineyard, do not glean what is left; it shall be for the alien, the orphan, and the widow... Remember that you were a slave in the land of Egypt; therefore, I am commanding you to do this. Deut 24:19-22, NRSV

No long forms to fill out. No inquisition. No stigma. Go to the fields following the reaper and take what you need.

"As it happened, Ruth came to the part of the field belonging to Boaz" (Ruth 2:3, NRSV). As it happened? A playful choice of words, perhaps? Or planning? Or providence?

There, Boaz notices Ruth among the gleaners. "Who is she?" he asks his workers. She is a Moabite, the one who came back with Naomi. She has been on her feet from early morning without resting, diligent as can be (Ruth 2:5-7).

Boaz invites Ruth to continue to glean in his fields, to help herself from the water jar at any time. He forbids any of his workers to molest Ruth, as vulnerable as she is, and he gives her an extra portion of barley. Then he gives her this blessing – "May the Lord reward you for deeds, and may you have a full reward from the Lord, the God of Israel, under whose wings you have come for refuge!" (Ruth 2:12, NRSV). Boaz then offers yet more kindness. What is going on here?

Naomi devises a plan to secure their future. This plan is full of sexual overtones and images of seduction, though these only lurk in the background of the story. Naomi instructs Ruth:

> My daughter, I need to seek some security for you, so that it may be well with you. Now here is our kinsman Boaz...Now wash and anoint yourself, and put on your best clothes and go down to the threshing floor; but do not make yourself known to the man until he has finished eating and drinking. When he lies down, observe the place where he lies; then go and uncover his feet and lie down; and he will tell you what to do. (Ruth 3:1-4, NRSV)

Off goes Ruth to carry out the plan. "When Boaz had eaten and drunk, and he was in a contented mood, he went to lie down at the end of the heap of grain. Then she came stealthily and uncovered his feet, and lay down. At midnight the man was startled, and turned over, and there, lying at his feet was a woman! He said, 'who are you?' and she answered, 'I am Ruth, your servant; spread your cloak over your servant, for you are next-of-kin' " (Ruth 3:7-9, NRSV).

To "uncover his feet" is probably a euphemistic way of saying, "to uncover his genitals." To "spread your cloak over your maidservant" echoes descriptions of betrothal. Naomi, through Ruth, confronts Boaz with his kinship obligations. There is no direct indication from this story of sexual consummation, but it was probably assumed.

Boaz acknowledges that Ruth has done the proper thing, and he promises to call an assembly of the people to tell them that Ruth is a worthy woman.

There is a further complication to this story. There is a nearer relative than Boaz, who is staking a claim to the land which belonged to Elimelech, husband to Naomi. By law, he has the "first right to redemption." But to claim this land, he must marry Ruth. She comes with the deal. That is more than this relative had bargained for. She is a Moabite, isn't she? No, I really can't do this. It could damage my own inheritance. No, you can have her (Ruth 4:6).

The way is cleared for Boaz to marry Ruth. "So Boaz took Ruth and she became his wife. When they came together, the Lord made her conceive, and she bore a son" (Ruth 4:13, NRSV). The future is now secure for both Naomi and Ruth. But this moment will send ripples far into the future – and even to us.

The concluding verses of the Book of Ruth are quite remarkable and not at all what one might expect in that very patriarchal world. There is a very counter-cultural story unfolding here. The women of the village take center stage. First, they sing a doxology to God – "Blessed be the Lord, who has not left you this day without next-of-kin; and may his name be renowned in Israel" (Ruth 4:14, NRSV). This is all very normal, and good, and proper, and socially acceptable. But then the women lavish praise on Ruth. They say to Naomi, "for your daughter-in-law who loves you, who is more to you than seven sons, has borne him" (4:15, NRSV). More than seven sons? In a culture where everything revolves around sons! The last thing the women of the village do is quite astounding. They name the baby, but not at all in the usual way. "The women of the neighbourhood gave him a name, saying, 'a son has been born to Naomi' " (Ruth 4:17, NRSV). Not born to the male line. Not born to Boaz. Born to Naomi.

"They named him Obed; he became the father of Jesse, the father of David" (Ruth 4:17, NRSV). And – he was the ancestor of Jesus. Just imagine what it means that Jesus descended from a lineage that started with a foreigner – a Moabite.

Afterword

The story of Ruth is the story of a foreign woman brought into the heart of the story of the people of Israel and of the coming of Jesus. It is the story of the deep love bond between Naomi, the mother-in-law, and Ruth. It is the story of delightful sexual scheming.

Underneath this marvellous story are glimpses of radical social change. The story creeps under the skin. It challenges and confronts the social norms of racial prejudice. It invites a bigger vision of how God works in our world. It is an answer to and challenge of Ezra's narrow exclusivism in expelling the foreign wives of the returned exiles. It challenges the rigidity of the patriarchal system. "More than seven sons" indeed. The story is wonderfully subversive.

There you have it: a story of redemption, love, sex and of confronting. And it's in the Bible.

Part Three
Exploring Contemporary Questions Around Human Sexuality

Part II focused on biblical stories where human sexuality played a major role, looking at stories which depicted both healthy sexuality but also stories which depicted abusive sexuality. In this next section, I focus more on our contemporary world and some of the choices we face in terms of living together in community as sexual beings – both in society and in the church. Hopefully, I continue to be faithful to what the Bible says, but I want to pay attention to what we name as "issues" in our world and in the church and to the way we experience ourselves as sexual beings in our culture and time. There is a lot of confusion around what the Bible says and there are various ways in which the church has interpreted those teachings. These sermons try to help congregants to navigate their contemporary questions around human sexuality in dialogue with the biblical text.

A Biblical Perspective on Human Sexuality

Sermon 11: October 18, 1992

1 Corinthians 6:12-20; Genesis 1 & 2; Psalm 139:12-13

> For it was you who formed my inward parts; you knit me together in my mother's womb. I praise you, for I am fearfully and wonderfully made. Wonderful are your works; that I know very well. My frame was not hidden from you, when I was being made in secret, intricately woven in the depths of the earth. Your eyes beheld my unformed substance. In your book were written, every one of them, all the days that were formed for me, when as yet there was none of them as yet existed. How weighty to me are your thoughts, O God! How vast is the sum of them.
>
> Psalm 139:13-17, NRSV

You and I are sexual beings. We were created that way by God. And God announced that this was very good (Genesis 1). Sexuality involves all that comes to mind when someone says, either

"I am female" or "I am male" – or "I am both." Sexuality refers to more than sex organs and to much more than sexual intercourse. It is a way of living in a body as a person with sexual drives. Our sexuality plays a huge role in our way of thinking, in how we feel and in how we act. In fact, we can never not be sexual beings. Our sexuality is a good gift from God. But it has sometimes been hard to talk about sexuality and about sex in the church. We have not always known how to talk about our bodies and about sex in a Christian way.

David Augsburger writes about our need to accept that our bodies are the "handiwork of God."

> Not evil in themselves, but good. Bodies are good, you would never want to be without one. Bodies are respectable. Some of the best Christians that I know have bodies. Bodies are useful. It's the only low-cost housing made by unskilled labor that progress can't improve. When God entered our world, He wasn't embarrassed to do it in a body. When Christ lived, taught, died and rose to life again, he did it in a body.[1]

Biblical Perspectives

My assignment today is to give some biblical perspective on human sexuality. What does the Bible say about sex? A good deal, it turns out. The Bible is anything but silent about a topic that we tend to be more silent about in the church.

The Bible talks about the broader topic of sexuality and the narrower topic of sex. It does so very straightforwardly, with no hint of embarrassment. The Bible covers both uses and abuses of God's good gifts — about intercourse, nakedness, a "sexual covenant," rape, adultery, fornication.

One of the challenges facing us in seeking the wisdom of

the Bible on these topics is the time gap and the culture gap between then and now. We live in a sex-titillated and sex-saturated society. We have made sex a very "big" thing – but in a way that often makes sex a very "small" thing, a primarily physical, biological thing. We have let all the hormones out of Pandora's box at once and don't know how to get out of that stampede without enormous damage being done. And for some reason, we find it difficult to talk about sex in church.

The culture of the biblical patriarchs was very different than ours. It, of course, wasn't an ideal recreation of Eden either. Their understanding of marriage was very different than ours is. Marriages were "arranged." Love could come after marriage and wasn't really essential to a good marriage. Some of the patriarchs had more than one wife, which does not seem to be critiqued by Scripture. Some, like Jacob, took mistresses from among their maidservants. And sometimes these patriarchs treated their wives and mistresses rather badly – note the story of Abraham and his mistress Hagar. We can, though, make some important affirmations about what the Bible says about human sexuality and about sexual expression.

Our bodies, and we as sexual beings, were created by God. Sex and sexuality are an integral part of God's good creation.

> So, God created humankind in his image, in the image of God he created them, male and female he created them... God saw everything that he had made, and indeed, it was very good.
> Gen 1:27, 31a, NRSV

This affirmation that our bodies are good, that our sexuality is a good gift from God, has been a bit hard for some Christians to make. I blame that on the Greeks and the Romans. They divided the universe into opposing forces – the spiritual realm and the material realm. It was a neat dualism. Humans were believed to have a soul and a body – a higher and a lower nature. The body was a prison of the soul, which was in constant battle against the temptations and weaknesses of the flesh. Humans must work to tame the body and its desires so that the soul can escape bodily corruption.[2]

This dualism was not there in the Old and New Testaments. There, the understanding of being human was much more holistic. Later, Christians were very much influenced by Greek and Roman thought – that is, Gnosticism. Augustine of Hippo, for example, one of the most influential early Christian teachers, was so influenced by dualism that he taught that sexual intercourse was the greatest threat to spirituality.[3] Intercourse was only for the sake of procreation – only for the sake of having children, and it should be engaged in only in a manner which does not bring sexual pleasure. Men should love their wives' souls, but they should hate their wives' bodies.

Our society too has been visited by this "dualism," but perhaps in the opposite direction – loving each other's bodies but neglecting the inner core of who we are. We may do very destructive and bizarre things to our bodies in order to conform to current notions of being sexy, thin, youthful, and glamorous. Our focus is more on outer beauty than it is on inner beauty. And so, there is a chasm between body and soul. Our bodies can go about having sexual encounters quite apart from an emotional commitment to the other, but when body and soul are not brought together, there is an opening for abuse to begin.

The Bible has a much healthier view of the human body than did the Romans or the Greeks. You could not split body and spirit apart. You were one whole being. A biblical view of the body affirms the goodness of our bodies in their femaleness and maleness. It will invite men and women to claim the blessedness of being created in the image of God. It will celebrate the rich variety of body shapes and sizes. And it will insist that we are whole, united persons, body and spirit together, the miracle of God's good creation.

The Bible also speaks about the purpose of our being made as sexual beings. One purpose for sexuality and marriage was to produce children. The first creation account in Genesis 1 says that God commanded the people to populate the earth. "God blessed them, [Adam and Eve] and God said to them, 'Be fruitful and multiply, and fill the earth and subdue it' " (Gen 1:28, NRSV). It was assumed by the Israelites that essentially every person, male and female, would get married and have children. Our modern notions of love were not essential in a marriage. Not having children was a tragedy. Marriage was, first of all, to produce children. Sex was, first of all, to produce children. ***Fruitfulness — the first creation account.***

But there is a second creation account in Genesis 2, which doesn't even mention reproduction as the purpose for being created male and female.

> Then the LORD God said, "It is not good that the man should be alone; I will make him a helper as his partner." ... So the LORD God caused a deep sleep to fall upon the man, and he slept; then he took one of his ribs and closed up its place with flesh. And the rib that the LORD God had taken from the man he made into a woman and brought her to the man. Then the man said, "This at last is bone of my bones and flesh of my flesh; this one shall be called Woman..." Therefore a man leaves his father and his mother and clings to his wife, and they become one flesh. And the man and his wife were both naked, and were not ashamed.
>
> Gen 2:18-25, NRSV

Here, the purpose of sex is companionship. Here, sexuality is seen as the means for a joyous expression of love. Here, sexual expression is a form of intimacy, of relationship – a bond of love. What is pictured here, I think, is a very wholesome, holistic recognition that intimate sexuality is a wonderful part of the way God created the bond between marriage partners. **Companionship and pleasure — the second creation account.**

The Bible does have some clear boundaries around sexual expression. Every culture has its boundaries. Our marriage act here in Ontario has a whole list of people we are not allowed to marry. For example, we cannot marry a close relative. These boundaries protect our community, our health, and what we value as families. There are some people you just are not supposed to have sex with. Our culture is in transition on this, and our assumed boundaries are being challenged. But boundaries there are.

The Bible isn't totally unified about its boundaries. And these boundaries do change over the many years of the writing of our Bible. Earlier, you could marry more than one wife. And you could have intercourse with your maidservants if the purpose was to produce children. If your brother were to die before his wife had children, it could be your obligation, your sacred duty, to have intercourse with her so that she too could have children.

There are also some earlier stories in the Old Testament where a man has sex with a prostitute, and there is very little judgement implied. But for the most part, sexual boundaries are placed around the home. Genital sexual expression belongs only within covenanted relationships. Throughout the Bible, there is a very strong condemnation of adultery. The New

Testament offers a strong condemnation for what it names as fornication, meaning sexual intercourse outside of marriage. ***Fruitfulness and pleasure — the first and second account.***

1 Cor 6:12-20

One of the biblical texts that speak about fornication very directly is 1 Corinthians 6. I want you to notice the argument that Paul makes here.

> Do you not know that your bodies are members of Christ? Should I therefore take the members of Christ and make them members of a prostitute? Never! Do you not know that whoever is united to a prostitute becomes one body with her? For it is said, 'The two shall become one flesh.' But anyone united to the Lord becomes one spirit with him. Shun fornication!
>
> 1 Cor 6:15-18, NRSV

Sexual intercourse is so much more than only a physical thing, a bio-mechanical act that you can repeat with many partners. It is *becoming one*. It has the meaning of covenant built into it. It is an expression of a deep relationship. And when that relationship isn't there, the sex act is a violation of what God intended. Paul calls it fornication.

I understand Paul to say that sexual intercourse belongs within a covenanted relationship. Paul concludes this chapter by saying this: "Do you not know that your body is the temple of the Holy Spirit within you, which you have from God" (1 Cor 6:19, NRSV). His is a very high view of the human body.

Marriage

What has surprised me is that there is no record of marriage ceremonies in the Bible. None. No legal ceremony or even any religious ceremony. There are a number of references to weddings in the Bible, but nowhere is there any hint of what the wedding ceremony might have looked like. We do hear about the "Wedding at Cana" in the New Testament (John 2:1-12), but again, no actual ceremony is talked about. I have been puzzled by this absence. It may be that, especially in Old Testament times, there were no particular "Temple-held" ceremonies of marriage.

The story of Isaak and Rebekah may be an early template. The story simply says he brought Rebekah "into his mother Sarah's tent. He took Rebekah, and she became his wife; and he loved her" (Gen 24:67, NRSV).

It seems, at least early in the biblical story, that marriage happened with the first act of intercourse. The first intercourse was seen as so profound a bonding with another person that you now knew the couple as married – as husband and wife. No legal or religious ceremony was needed. As the Israelite story unfolded, there may have been a development of particular "ceremonies of marriage," but the Bible does not record them.

Intercourse

In the Old Testament, the word for intercourse is יָדַה (*yadah*), which means "to know someone." In the story of Isaak and Rebekah, the text simply records Isaak "knew" his wife and she bore him a son (Gen 4:25). Intercourse is "to know" the other – a deep knowing. So much more than only a physical act.

The Bible also uses the word *yadah* when it talks about

God "knowing" us, and for us "knowing" God. We are talking about a deep knowing. There is nothing shallow or casual about it. Intercourse which is not *"yadah"* which is shallow, is intercourse which may be abusive and exploitative. (NOTE: the word *yadah* will also be explained in a different context in Sermon 17, "Love in a Reflective Mode.")

Afterword

I want to make a concluding point about a biblical understanding of sexuality. All of the ideals are eventually given – the unity and wholeness of the human person; sex for procreation and companionship; boundaries within which sexual expression is appropriate; condemnation of adultery, fornication, rape, and incest; a high view of the human body; the "covenantal" nature of intercourse; treating each person, male and female, with full respect and dignity.

But the Bible also acknowledges our failure to fully live up to these ideals. Each of the patriarchs, heroes of the faith, messes with these ideals at some point. There is in the Bible what I would call a "pastoral perspective," which acknowledges how we humans mess up. What do you do when people fail, when they sin, when they break the ideals set forth?

Sexual sins, like all sins, are not unforgivable, though some sexual sins deeply violate another person and may leave lasting wounds. Healing and forgiveness are possible, even for King David who rapes Bathsheba and then kills her husband. And yet there were huge consequences and huge pain that cannot be erased.

We have probably all been wounded in our sexuality. We definitely all fall short of the ideals given us. We are all wounded in some way, and some of us are almost broken. We all need forgiveness and healing and a renewed vision for wholeness. In our sexually obsessive, genitally preoccupied society where the Other becomes an object and where we are often very abusive of each other, healing is hard to find.

Perhaps what we need is a sexual "counter-culture," one which gets its cues from the insights of the Scriptures, where personhood, dignity, and covenant notions form the basis of our healing. We do need to see our bodies, including our sexuality, as a wonderful gift from God, a temple of the Holy Spirit; we humans are made in the image of God. We honour that in ourselves – and in the Other. We can never "violate" the one we honour.

Our sexuality is a wonderful gift of God.

Intimacy and Power: The Ongoing Struggle
Sermon 12

Genesis 2

Bob and I have been friends for over 20 years. Since we live in different cities, we have a chance to visit only every three or four years. Bob is intense, unpredictable, and direct. He does not make small talk easily.

This August, on our way here to Toronto, our paths crossed again for a couple of hours. I have come to expect provocative, hard questions from him. When you visit with Bob, you decide very quickly either to enter into an intense, passionate conversation or stay on the surface of things and expect to say goodbye in 10 minutes. He will just up and leave.

The six of us had barely settled into our seats when it came. "Gary, why are so damned many Mennonite marriages breaking up these days? And why is it that you counsellor-types have the worst record of all?"

You can't anticipate Bob. Neither can you prepare for him. We floundered around for a while, searching here and there for answers.

- Maybe people don't have the same commitment to their spouse.
- Maybe our expectations for a fulfilling relationship are idealized beyond what is attainable, and we become dissatisfied with what we've got.
- Maybe the pressure is on young people today to get married to the wrong people for all the wrong reasons – how can we know what love means when we are saturated with romantic illusions?
- Maybe we haven't learned to face real conflict, and we run away when differences emerge.
- Maybe we are so programmed to self-fulfilment and self-gratification that we'd rather change than continue with the routine phases of a relationship.
- Maybe some people just can't be lived with.
- Maybe all kinds of things.

We went on to other equally absorbing topics, feeling just a bit dissatisfied with the answers ventured. We had a good go at the church and whether or not it was at all relevant to life in a modern world. His friends were dropping out, he said. We even talked about giving ourselves "permission to mourn" when someone close to us dies.

When all at once, out of the blue, not knowing what I said, I blurted out, "It's because we haven't resolved the two issues of intimacy and power. Every marriage has to deal with the questions of intimacy and power. If you don't resolve those two key issues in a satisfactory way, your marriage will continue to struggle."

The Scope of the Issue

I'm still not sure I know what I'm talking about. I haven't been able to sort out the implications of the above insight. But my hunch is that how we come to terms with intimacy and power in our lives is at the heart of all our relationships and at the heart of the question of meaning in life.

I shared my half-baked insight with our preaching team (four laypersons selected by our congregation to assist in preaching and in choosing and developing themes). They pushed and pulled the idea in all kinds of directions. Soon we had a theme which we felt was big enough for at least three months of preaching. After all, one could explore the psychological aspect of the topic – intimacy and power in our relationships and in how we understand ourselves. There is surely also a profound sociological dimension – forces of intimacy and power at work in the home, the church, and especially in our society. But the heart of its theme for Christians may be theological in nature. How do we understand intimacy and power in terms of our images of God, in the passion stories of Jesus, and even in how we come to terms with death?

Marriage Stories

To get us in touch with the theme a bit more, I want to tell stories on the theme. The stories are about marriage: one contemporary, one biblical, but the theme is so much bigger than marriage. It is for the single person as much as for the married person, for the young as well as for the elderly.

Art and Ellen: Already sweethearts in grade nine, it was easy to see why Ellen had a crush on him. Art really was very handsome. He was a good athlete, easygoing, well-liked. He was the practical type, good at fixing things, and raced his dad's car around the country roads long before he was sixteen. Art wasn't very good at schoolwork, but then who needed English and social studies when you knew you were going to be a mechanic? He had already stripped down a car motor by the time he was 15.

And it was easy to see why he had a crush on her. Ellen was beautiful enough to draw whistles, and was an excellent dancer at the school social events, though, of course, that was frowned upon by her rural Mennonite church. She was reserved enough to have a quality of mystery about her. Her parents thought she bottled things up inside – didn't communicate much with them. She enjoyed schoolwork, though she hid her good marks from the rest of the kids and never let Art know her true intelligence.

Art and Ellen were the ideal couple, madly in love with each other, always together, and got married at age 19, the summer after high school graduation. Their daughter Teresa was born six months later. Two years later, Henry was born. They moved into the city because Art got a mechanic's job there, and they made some tentative attempts to connect with a Mennonite church in the city. But city church life seemed strange to them.

Ellen and Art were very happy – happily married, at least. Ellen stayed home with the kids. Art was the provider. He didn't much like domestic chores.

Life was following the right script, the script that was programmed into them from childhood. They both felt good when Ellen had a bedtime prayer with the kids.

· · ·

Ellen goes back to school: At age 27, Ellen took a course at the university. She was no longer fully content at home. She was restless. Sometimes she envied friends who had a career. Sometimes she found herself asking: "Am I only a wife and a mother? Who am I inside?"

After a second course the following year, Art put his foot down. "I don't want you taking any more courses. You're changing, and I don't like it. I come home, and supper's not on the table. Your nose is in the books."

Ellen said that she loved studying, that she felt cooped up in their relationship, that no way would she let him keep bossing her around, and that he shouldn't feel so threatened by her developing self. She wondered out loud once whether she really loved him anymore. She took three courses the next year and found daycare for her kids.

They were fighting more often now, and Art would clam up and sometimes storm out and head for the bar. Ellen cried a lot.

One evening, Art yelled, "You aren't the girl I got married to. I don't know who you are anymore." And he hit her.

Ellen left home that night.

Reviving Intimacy: Ellen did come back. And in wrenching pain, Ellen and Art struggled to revive a dead marriage. The issue was power, and it was intimacy. For a while, Art had exercised the power in their relationship. He was a macho man, a provider, in control. Then Ellen sought her own power. Studying was a way of getting out from under his control and developing her own strength. The problem was they weren't really intimate with each other – emotionally intimate.

Sex was often a power game, a substitute for intimacy.

They were afraid to share deeply their feelings, fears, and hopes. They were afraid of being vulnerable with each other.

And so, the question now, on the precipice, was whether they were willing to deal with the core issue. Could Art risk allowing his wife to grow and change and become her own person? Could he name his fears? Could Ellen risk communicating with him, sharing her fearful struggle for identity, her overwhelming guilt, her thirst for knowledge, her need for closeness and not just being the good wife? Could they give up their power game with each other, the striving to have power and control over the other?

They made it, after many tears. At 33, Art and Ellen had a marriage that was much stronger than it was at 19.

Adam and Eve: Intimate and Powerful

Genesis 1 and 2 state both the ideal of human relationships (intimacy) and the problem (power). Chapter 3 acknowledges the havoc that is created when a thirst for power overcomes a relationship.

There are two creation stories. In Chapter 2, the second creation story focuses on closeness and intimacy. "It is not good for the man to be alone. I will make a helper suitable for him" (Gen 2:18). This is a remarkable passage about power too.

At a time when most societies on earth classed women as inferior, as an object to be owned by the husband for his comfort and pleasure, the Hebrews ideally gave her a position of equality (though, in reality, they often missed that goal). She was to be a partner, an equal helpmate, a companion, of the same stuff and worth as men.

A man and woman would find in each other a relationship so rich and so satisfying that all other relationships, including their father and mother, would be less important. The two people would become one. The relationship would be mutually satisfying to both spouses.

The first creation story in Genesis 1 says clearly, "So God created humankind in his image, in the image of God he created them; male and female he created them" (Gen 1:27, NRSV). And the point of the second story from Genesis 2 is their similarity, their companionship – "Bone of my bones and flesh of my flesh" (Gen 2:23, NRSV). They become one flesh.

The word picture painted is an idyllic one. There, in the Garden of Eden, Adam and Eve find closeness to nature, closeness to each other, closeness to God. They know true intimacy.

And the writer comments, "the man and his wife were both naked, and were not ashamed" (Gen 2:25, NRSV).

The Power Temptation

In chapter three of Genesis, there is an abrupt, harsh change.

> 'You will not die,' the serpent said to the woman... 'for God knows that when you eat of [the forbidden tree] your eyes will be opened, and you will be like God, knowing good and evil.'
>
> Gen 3:4-5, NRSV

God is just playing games with you, woman. He wants to keep all his power to himself.

And Eve is sorely tempted. To have power like God has, that would be something special. To be like God and to fully know good and evil, what a surge of excitement just to think of it.

And Adam is tempted as much as Eve. Adam too is tempted to trade intimacy for power. "Fine life here in this old garden, what with all the food and the beautiful wife, but wouldn't it be something to really have control in this place and not just live here."

And in their quest for power, intimacy is destroyed. They blame each other. They are now against each other. Their closeness with each other is gone. They try to hide from God. Their closeness with God is gone. They struggle with the land and lose Eden. Their closeness with nature is also gone.

Origin of Shame

And the commentator makes a big point of the fact that now they suddenly realize that they are naked, and it is a thing of shame to them, which it wasn't before. That point tells a powerful truth, for in genuine intimacy, there is no shame. In abusive power struggles, there is no intimacy, only shame.

Afterword

Adam and Eve are universalized humans relating to each other as sexual beings. We realize that the same struggles and the same temptations are ours.

Within each of us is a deep need for intimacy, for being close to others, for a depth-sharing of who we are with others. We can live without marriage. We can live without sexual intercourse. We cannot survive as healthy human beings without closeness.

But within each of us, there is also a striving for power. We would like to be in control, both of ourselves and of others. We too like to act like God. But our power trips will always drive us out of the Garden of Eden.

In the ongoing struggle between power and intimacy in our own lives, know that when power wins, intimacy always loses, but when intimacy wins, power is shared.

Accountability, Priests, Prophets and Sages

Sermon 13: September 8, 2002

Foundations for our Study of Human Sexuality

Matthew 16:13-20; Jeremiah 18:18; Matthew 23:34

I come a bit reluctantly to the end of summer. There is nothing more relaxing or renewing than to camp somewhere where God's beauty astounds me every day, and then in the dark evenings, I can stare into a campfire as long as I want. Even so, life does not really take a vacation. We cannot take vacation from life – only from work and from location. Within our congregation, people continue to experience sickness, healing, death of loved ones, celebrations, crises, opportunities, and just very ordinary living. I experienced a bit of a crisis myself on Thursday. I was doing some house painting late in the evening and managed to overturn my paint container onto our bedroom carpet.

But fall is here. Our summer hiatus is over. Today, we begin the second phase of our process of discernment around human sexuality, with a particular focus on homosexuality. Through the fall, we want to engage in a serious, in-depth study of biblical, theological, and contemporary questions around our understanding of human sexuality. As we begin phase two of this study and discernment, I want to issue an invitation, a warning, a comfort, and a challenge.

The INVITATION. I invite each of you, whether a regular attendee, guest, or church shopper, to enter the study process. I think it will be a wonderful learning opportunity. We did not choose it. Perhaps we did not want it. But God is giving it to us. David Schroeder, retired professor of New Testament at Canadian Mennonite Bible College, writes:

> I believe the Spirit of God brings things to the surface for the church to address when the church is ready. It is the same in our personal lives. When we have suppressed things that are too difficult for us to handle, they arise to consciousness at a time we are able to deal with them... I have faith that the church is now ready to deal with homosexuality in a way that avoids either-or-solutions of inclusion or exclusion.[1]

I invite you to enter this season of learning with an open mind and open heart, anticipating that the Spirit of God will attend to us and direct us.

But I also issue a WARNING. You need to know that we will be engaged in this process for some months to come. We want to do it thoroughly. There is no avoiding it here. Be forewarned. But I also want to warn you that any serious Bible study is dangerous business. We might learn something new. We might learn something that challenges what we thought we knew. If you come grimly holding on to long-cherished interpretations or biases, the Spirit of God might have to work extra hard to penetrate your life. But she will.

A word of COMFORT. During most Sunday morning worship services, you probably won't even hear the words "sexuality" or "homosexuality." Sunday morning is for worship. It is for singing and praying and being renewed, forming community, and meeting God in a way that changes us. The sermons over the next while are meant to provide frameworks for understanding the Scriptures, foundations for the way the Bible can shape our lives and our ethics. It is in the Sunday School hour afterwards that the specific texts and topics around sexuality will be dealt with. The sermon and the class are meant to fit together, but the sermon will be more foundational than specific. So be comforted. The worship service will be for worship. And be comforted knowing that God will be with us through our journey, through our struggles, through our conflicts, and through our praying together.

Finally, a word of CHALLENGE. I challenge us all to give burial to the totally dysfunctional categories "liberal" and "conservative." On most topics, but especially around human sexuality, I think that neither a bland liberal acceptance nor a harsh conservative literalness will cut it. Both boxes are far too limiting and stifling. The Gospel of Jesus Christ has always called for a third way, a new way, often an upside-down way of seeing the reality of God and of God's will for us. We will seek to be rigorous, biblically and theologically, and we will seek to be open to any new direction the Spirit of God will lead us into. Surely, the words conservative and liberal cannot contain what we need to learn.

How will we be church?

The question for us as we process the intriguing issues around how we understand our human sexuality will be, "How will we be church?" That will be even more basic than how we come out in our discernment at the end. How will we be church? How will we be church when dealing with a topic so troubling and so heated and so divisive? How will we be church when we disagree passionately with another's point of view? How will we be the body of Christ when the different parts of the body are not in tune with each other?

Controversial issues have never been absent from the church, either locally or universally. We need to think only of issues like divorce and remarriage, women in ministry, interracial marriage, slavery for that matter, paying war taxes, or how we, as Mennonites, understand our peace position. Sometimes the church has been almost torn apart by these issues. Sometimes it has barely muddled through. And sometimes there has been new growth and new unity. What makes the difference? How can we be church in such a way that we will grow in community and grow in Christ as we dialogue with each other about the questions surrounding our sexuality?

Foundations

I want to work with two foundational frameworks here, which have been very important in our Anabaptist heritage. They offer a particular perspective on how to be the church, especially when there is conflict.

1) The church is a binding and loosing community.

2) We need to listen to the voices of priests, the prophets and the sages – and then bring all of this to God in worship.

Foundation 1: The church is a binding and loosing community

Central to how the Anabaptists understood church was that it was a binding and loosing community. That is how they read Matthew 16 and 18. I am indebted to Dr. David Schroeder for his interpretation of these texts.[2] I will work primarily with Matthew chapter 16.

We enter this text through the story of the confession of Peter. It has finally become clear to Peter. Jesus is, in fact, the Christ. Jesus said to the disciples, " 'But who do you say that I am?' Simon Peter answered, 'You are the Messiah, the son of the living God' " (Matt 16:15-16, NRSV).

Responding to this confession, Jesus says:

And I tell you, you are Peter, and on this rock, I will build my church, and the gates of Hades will not prevail against it. I will give you the keys of the Kingdom of Heaven, and whatever you bind on earth will be bound in heaven, and whatever you loose on earth will be loosed in heaven.

Matt 16:18-19, NRSV

There are three pieces of this text I want to focus on.

1. *And I tell you, you are Peter, and on this rock, I will build my church.* I think that Peter himself is not the rock. The rock is Peter's confession, that Jesus is the Messiah, the son of the living God. It is Peter who is the first one to make this confession. There is a play on words here, I think. Petra means rock, and the name "Peter" comes from the root word for rock. But I think that it is Peter's confession that Jesus is the Christ which is the foundation for the church – not Peter himself.[3]

Permit a small digression: In Sudbury, where I took part in an ecumenical ministerial association, there was a United Church built on the solid rock of Sudbury and was, in fact, named "St. Peter's on-the-Rock." I was impressed. I asked the pastor about the theological meaning of the church's name. "Theological!?" he snorted. "We name it 'St. Peter's on the rocks' – It is a financial statement."

Peter's confession that Jesus is really the Christ means that anyone and everyone who confesses that Jesus is the Messiah, the Son of the living God, is a part of the church and thus they are my brother or sister in Christ – even if they think and believe very differently than I on basic things – even if they do not understand Jesus' words of being peacemakers and loving enemies in the passionate way I do – even if their ethical standards are different than mine – even if they read the Scriptures differently than I do. The church is built on the confession that Jesus is the Messiah, the Christ, the Son of the living God. Everyone who makes that confession is my brother or my sister in Christ. Period.

2. *I will give you the keys of the kingdom of heaven.* Keys were given to a steward of the house. The steward had the authority to open doors and to shut doors, to invite people in and to assure the safety of the house by keeping some people out. In this text, the keys of the Kingdom are given to one person, Peter. Some churches, like the Catholic church, have made much of this, suggesting that church leaders (such as popes, bishops, etc.) have the power and responsibility to keep the church pure. In Matthew 18, a kind of parallel passage, the task of being a steward-gatekeeper is given to all the disciples. It is really given to the whole church. And it seems to me that the Holy Spirit kept challenging the church to use those keys for opening the doors of the church rather than to lock the doors.

3. *Whatever you bind on earth will be bound in heaven, and whatever you loose on earth will be loosed in heaven.* The words "loose" and "bind" would have been clearly understood in Judaism. In Judaism, it was the scribes who interpreted the "Law" for the people. Their function was to "loose" you or "bind" you to an interpretation of the Law. They translated the general commands of the Law into the specifics of everyday life. They made judgments about what was permitted and what was not permitted. When a full majority of the scribes agreed on an interpretation, then it became binding on the whole community and was considered ratified in heaven. Many times it took years, decades, or even centuries for such an authentic majority to occur. Till then, an interpretation was not fully binding. To the disciples of Jesus, and now to the church, was given the challenge of making discernments about how to interpret the law of God, the challenge of "binding and loosing" – setting people free from something or binding them to an understanding.

What is the church's "loosing" task today? In simple terms, it is to partner with God in setting people free – free from whatever enslaves them. Free from the prejudices, addictions, powers, and forces that hold us back from living and loving fully.

But in this loosing, a "freeing God" is also a "binding God." That is the story of the people of Israel. After being set free from slavery, God invited these freed people into a covenant relationship, and gave them the Ten Commandments. It is a "loosing" and a "binding." God sets the people free, and invites them into a covenant that is binding. You shall have no other gods before me... you shall not steal or murder or commit adultery. You bind yourselves to God and to the community. You bind yourselves to what gives life – to what is life-giving.

Jesus lived out this loosing-and-binding character of God. Even the name "Jesus" has at its root a word that means "to become broad" or "to set free." Jesus was the freeing, loosing, saving one. So often, Jesus challenged the scribes for emphasizing too much the binding part of their role – and neglecting the loosing part. He said that the scribes bound people with heavy burdens (Matt 23:4) – but did nothing to set people free. Jesus came to free people from the bondage of heavy interpretations of the law. Jesus went about freeing people and healing people. Amazingly, women became free to follow Jesus. Foreigners were invited in. Outsiders became insiders.

In Matthew 16 and 18, Jesus gives the mandate of loosing and binding to Peter, to the disciples, and to the whole church. It is an awesome responsibility. It means that the church is meant to be a moral community helping to make discernments about ethics and morals. It is not good enough to say that ethics is a private affair that doesn't concern the community.

It also means, in my view, that it is the whole church, not only its leaders, pastors, biblical scholars, or the denominational organization, that must be engaged in the binding and the loosing. We here at TUMC have to engage in the process of discernment around differing ways of expressing our sexuality in relationships. We have to hear each voice in the congregation. We have to be open to the leading of God's Spirit.

We don't know the measure or scope of our loosing and binding, but I believe that if we do this under God's guidance, it will lead us in the direction of life and freedom.

It may just take us much longer than we want it to. Sometimes it took decades, even longer, for the scribes to reach an agreement on an interpretation. We leave it to God's time and in the meanwhile, we commit ourselves to each other for the duration, committed to being the church in our disagreements with each other, living and moving and discerning in the name of, and in the Spirit of, Christ.

Foundation 2: Listening to Priests, Prophets and Sages

> Then they said, 'Come, let us make plots against Jeremiah —
> for instruction shall not perish from the priest, nor counsel
> from the wise [sage], nor the word from the prophet. Come,
> let us bring charges against him, and let us not heed any of
> his words.'
> Jer 18:18, NRSV

The Israelites knew that the Scriptures themselves contained different kinds of writings, which, when combined, gave a full sense of God's interaction with humans. They knew that the priest, sage, and prophet represented three very different kinds of interaction with sacred Scripture.[4] They knew that all were needed in learning to live a faithful life in the presence of their God. (Some examples of how priests, prophets, and sages functioned will be explored more fully in the appendix 'An Essay on Homosexuality'). Here is a concise summary of their respective roles:

The **priest** represented the tradition, the foundations, the core story of faith. The **prophet** challenged individuals and the community toward transformation and change. The **sage** was the wise person who brought to bear the wisdom of the world.

Priest, prophet, sage. Each of them has important things to say to us about human sexuality, and perhaps specifically to our discernment around homosexuality. In the priests among us, we have the foundational, identity-forming basics. In the prophets among us, we have challenging, rethinking of stuff. In the sages among us, we have wisdom and practical ways of thinking. We need to listen to all three. They mirror the threefold form of the "Hebrew canon" of Scripture: *Torah*-Law, *Neviim*-Prophets and *Ketuvim*-Wisdom writings.

What gives me hope and excitement about our process and our study is that I think we have good people resources in each of these areas. We have people who can present the foundational traditions to us. We certainly have the people who can challenge us with a disruptive prophetic voice. And we have many wise people full of a huge amount of knowledge to share with us. May we hear them all.

Afterword

There is one other kind of Scripture which does not precisely fit into the other three I have listed. That is worship. It is the Psalms. It is the prayers. It is the direct speech of humans to God. Songs, prayers of lament, of pain, of praise. They arise out of the conviction that God is indeed with God's people and that God longs for communion with us. Worship binds everything together. Worship brings priest-prophet-sage under one common human need – to commune with God and to be renewed personally and communally.

In worship, we acknowledge our need for God and our own inadequate understanding of the Bible, our lives, and our sexuality. In worship, we become one even as we disagree with each other. In worship, we seek a new word from God. For us as Christians, newer understandings of human sexuality must be discerned in the context of prayer and worship.

I pray that our community will be nourished and nurtured and unified by worship as we continue the hard work of studying, learning, and engaging each other around the topic of our sexuality and as we try to discern God's will for us.

How will we be church? By praying together as we engage in the awesome process of binding and loosing, as we hear the Word of God and the words of priest, prophet, and sage. May we engage each other truthfully and lovingly around the questions about our human sexuality and how we respond to each other in the church with our different sexual natures.

Part Four
Weddings and Marriage

I must acknowledge that I have always enjoyed marriage preparation with couples preparing for their wedding – and officiating weddings.

I did hear from pastors and priests in the more mainline traditions that they sometimes dreaded "wedding season." They felt almost overwhelmed with the large number of weddings they were asked to officiate, often with couples only loosely connected to the church they were leading and whom they didn't really know. "It feels like I am running a marriage mill," I heard from some pastors and priests. I did have one year in Edmonton when I officiated eight weddings. But usually, there were less than that. I had ample time and energy to lead and enjoy a longer marriage preparation time and wedding preparation time. I looked forward to helping couples reflect on the challenges and opportunities of their relationship, and then to plan a wedding service together with them, which would reflect who they were and would celebrate their commitment to each other.

In 1980, Faith and Life Press and Mennonite Publishing House invited Lydia and me to write a "Wedding Booklet," which would include the meaning of the wedding, the process of planning the wedding service and attendant functions, and the role of the officiating minister.[1] The booklet invited ministers to work with couples in planning a creative service that reflected who the couple was and expressed their hopes for their marriage. At that time, Lydia was not able to give time to this project. She also felt that her experience was not as a minister, so I did the writing. To my surprise – and delight – when the booklet was published, Lydia was named as co-author. We have continued to work together, sometimes in the pre-marriage counselling and occasionally at the wedding itself.

I begin this section with an article reprinted from *Vision* that Lydia and I wrote together about weddings during a semester at Anabaptist Mennonite Biblical Seminary. We were intrigued by the changing wedding patterns, and so we researched various approaches to weddings. Since then, new patterns have emerged, but many couples still ask the pastor to preach a "short" sermon at their wedding celebration. I include a selection of these sermons that I have preached over the years.

Sexuality in the Wedding
Reflection 14: Gary and Lydia

by Gary Harder & Lydia Neufeld Harder[1]

Genesis 1 & 3, Song of Songs

The rules of the sexual dance have been changing rapidly in our society. No longer do most couples look to the church for permission, via a marriage license, to dance together sexually. Pastors no longer oversee the dance floor. However, many couples still come to pastors to preside at their weddings. They still come to the church to marry – and perhaps to look for deeper meanings for their married and sexual lives. How will we respond? How do we negotiate the changing dance floor scene?

Reflections from the dance floor (Gary)

I am all too aware of the overt sexuality she exudes. It frightens and disconcerts me a bit. It excites me, enough, at least, to know that I need to keep my boundaries clearly in place. "Don't start fantasizing," I order myself. How then to begin the marriage preparation journey for this couple sitting before me? Especially when I know we will need to talk about their sexuality.

Jan and Eric (not their real names) have come to my office because they want me to officiate at their wedding. They come hesitantly. They bring guilty feelings. They have been living together for almost a year and cannot reconcile that fact with their upbringing and stated convictions that full sexual expression belongs only within marriage. They are Christians, and they feel they have betrayed their Christian commitment. They are tired of hiding their living arrangement from their families, and they want to commit their lives to each other in marriage.

I can see how Eric might have succumbed to Jan's sexual appeal – and, for that matter, how Jan could have been attracted to Eric's strong aura of maleness. They start listing excuses for moving in together. There were economic realities. They already knew they wanted to get married, so they just started having sex a bit early. And then Jan is in tears. "Can we still get married in the church? Will you still marry us?"

In some ways, the church has seen the marriage license as a license to have sex. The wedding service legitimates full sexual expression. Marriage is the boundary that regulates our sexuality. Before marriage, sex is bad. After marriage, sex is legitimated – almost regardless of how it is expressed. We have had a hard time naming sexual abuse within marriage.

But we find it difficult to be honest about sex in marriage preparation and in the wedding service. It hovers just beneath the surface, bubbling away just out of reach of words, unnamed until someone tells a crude joke at the reception and leaves most of us embarrassed. In the way we do weddings, can we somehow deal honestly and compassionately with sexuality? Can we address sex with integrity, aware of the highly sexualized nature of our society, aware of how our society commodifies sexuality? Can we be ready to offer a wholesome vision of sexual expression?

Perhaps integrity around our sexuality is a gift the church can offer a couple getting married. But then we will have to get our act together. We have to be open about sex in the church. We have to talk about it. We have to name the blessing and the curse, how sex can wonderfully enrich our lives and how it can harm us and empty our relationships of meaning. We have to struggle as a church to understand and own our vision for healthy sexuality. And we need to pass on our vision to our children.

But how do we make our sexuality sacred, a part of our journey with and toward God? How do we resist letting our secular society control our understanding of sexuality?

From colleagues in ministry, I have heard about three possible ways of responding to a common-law couple wanting to get married. Some pastors start with rules, insisting that the couple move apart and refrain from intercourse until the wedding. Others try to ignore the issue, believing that if they don't ask, they won't have to deal with it. Others try to engage the couple about their sexual expression as honestly as they can and, from there, point to a fuller, covenanted vision.

The Bible is more forthright about human sexuality than we are often able to be. Let's consider Genesis 1 and 3.

In pleasure and delight, God breathes life and spirit into the human beings. "I have created relating beings," exults God, "loving beings, male and female beings. Companionship and intimacy can replace loneliness and alienation."

God delights in seeing Adam and Eve enjoy the garden, each other's companionship, and conversation with their Creator. The woman and man tend the garden, name the animals, run free and naked and unashamed, taking pleasure in each other's love and in each other's bodies. And God laughs with them in joy.

But alas, other powers also reside in the garden and in each psyche. Another spirit breathes an unwelcome discordant reality into Eden. These first mythical humans, like each of us, have a lust for power, perhaps the strongest urge of all. Power. Control. Avoidance of vulnerability. Wanting to be like God, knowing good and evil, they eat of the fruit of the forbidden tree.

Then comes the blaming. And denial. And defending the indefensible. And exploitation. And hiding from God and from each other. All hell breaks loose as they are chased out of the garden.

The intimacy is lost. These first humans are alienated from each other and from God. Their nakedness is now a source of shame, and they cover their sexual parts. In their nakedness, Eden slips out of their grasp. But is it lost forever?

If we are honest with ourselves, we will acknowledge that many of the couples – maybe even the majority – that we marry in the church are not virgins on their wedding night. We are a long way from Eden. What do we do with that reality?

Integrity starts with candour in the office, with being honest with the couple wanting to get married. Far better to deal with the reality of the couple living together before marriage than to pretend, white wedding dress notwithstanding, that they are "pure." I thank Eric and Jan for being so open and honest with me. "I think we can now talk candidly about what your living together has meant for your relationship. And my hope is that it can lead to a wedding service that has integrity."

We are now free to explore a more full-orbed vision of intimacy. Jan and Eric acknowledge that their sex drives have taken over their relationship and that they are struggling to find other intimate ways to relate to each other. They are not able to keep in touch with each other emotionally as well as they want to. They have not explored how they could include spiritual intimacy in their relationship, even though both are Christians and regularly attend church. Their friendship and social networks are not well developed. Perhaps their guilt about their living arrangement is an inhibiting factor. They are dissatisfied with various aspects of their relationship. Even their sex life is less than satisfying. Will getting married magically heal their relationship?

Marriage can contribute to healing, but not without hard work. Jan and Eric drink in that bigger picture of intimacy. Over time, they begin to address areas that they have neglected in their haste to move in together. They begin to be more vulnerable to each other emotionally. They even start praying together, one of the hardest kinds of closeness to embrace because it is so intensely intimate. I realize, as we explore this terrain in preparation for their marriage, that I am no longer conscious of the overt sexuality that first drew my notice on meeting Jan. As my relationship with her and Eric has deepened, other aspects of her identity now engage my attention.

Their wedding is honest and joyful. I can name before their families and communities their journey from living together to a relationship that is ready for the multifaceted intimacy of a healthy marriage. We freely reinsert sexuality into the service.

The Song of Songs revisits the wholesome sexuality of Eden. The song is a symphony of sensuality in five movements. It is unashamedly erotic. Gone is the violence and cover-up of a distorted Eden, replaced with a restored and full mutuality. The woman is as free as the man to make advances. Neither dominates nor exploits the other.

. . .

She begins the song, and he responds.

Let him kiss me with the kisses of his mouth! For your love is better than wine, your anointing oils are fragrant, Your name is perfume poured out... (Song of Solomon 1:2-4, NRSV)

I compare you, my love, to a mare among Pharaoh's chariots... (1:9)

My beloved is to me a bag of myrrh that lies between my breasts.

My beloved is to me a cluster of henna blossoms in the vineyards of En-gedi... (1:13-14)

Ah, you are beautiful, my love; ah, you are beautiful;

your eyes are doves. Ah, you are beautiful, my beloved, truly lovely... (1:15-16)

With great delight I sat in his shadow, and his fruit was sweet to my taste.

He brought me to the banqueting house, and his intention toward me was love... (2:3-4)

How beautiful you are, my love, how very beautiful,

Your eyes are doves behind your veil.

Your hair is like a flock of goats, moving down the slopes of Gilead... (4:1-2)

Your two breasts are like two fawns, twins of a gazelle, that feed among the lilies... (4:5)

My beloved is all radiant and ruddy, distinguished among ten thousand. His head is the finest gold; his locks are wavy, black as a raven. His eyes are like doves... (5:10-12) *His body is ivory work, encrusted with sapphires...* (5:14)

And finally, this symphony of sensuality ends, as it must. The curtain is drawn shut, and with it, the circle of intimacy between the two closes as they become one: *Make haste, my beloved, and be like a gazelle or a young stag upon the mountains of spices!* (Song of Solomon 8:14, NRSV)

· · ·

Earthy, embodied, erotic, sensual – a powerful yet tender love song written in a patriarchal context, revisiting old Eden and sending waves into ever-new Edens.

Jan and Eric's marriage is happy and honest, growing in the context of their congregation. They continue to learn that intimacy is God's gift to them and their gift to each other. One wonderful part of their many-faceted intimacy is enjoyment of each other's bodies in full sexual expression.

Musings from the Balcony (Lydia)

The balcony overlooks the dance floor, providing perspective on the unfolding sexual dance. The view from the balcony encourages us to reflect and ask, what is really happening here?

When I step back to reflect theologically on weddings and sexuality, I realize that most of the time I do not think about the wedding as "the liturgical ritualized celebration of the sexual union of two persons."[2] In fact, the words of the wedding service rarely speak about the mystery of sexual desire or the creative reproductive power of sexual union. Because the wedding is a worship service, we assume that the focus is on the spiritual and sacred covenant that is deeper and broader than having sex. However, what strikes me about our wedding services is that we often leave our sexuality at the church door. We have become so comfortable with separating the sacred and the secular as we enter worship that we don't even notice that no one is speaking about physical intimacy at an event in which it should be celebrated as a gift of God.

I wonder if this separation of the sacred and secular leaves us open to the seductive power of our technological culture. That culture wants to take over our most intimate relationships and make them shallow, artificial, and superficial. In our society, the perfect sexual relationship is a commodity that can be acquired with the right technique or through using the right beauty product or by having so-called safe sex or by planning the most romantic wedding. The market encourages couples to enjoy sexual goods without responsibility, without outside interference, and without the burdens of a community ethic. Marriage is available to anyone who wishes for it, and if one product does not suit, perhaps another will. The wedding is in danger of becoming a counterfeit, a spectacle produced for public consumption. Sexuality has been reduced to a possession rather than experienced as a gift of God which we tend and nourish through hard work.

In earlier times, we could not so easily ignore sexuality. If a couple lived together, a baby would likely appear before long. If a woman died in childbirth, her husband needed to find a new wife in order to provide a secure home for the children. If a young man bought a farm, he sought a wife to share the work with him. Partnership was built into the marriage relationship for economic and social reasons. Therefore, community rules could be effective in encouraging a deeper and more multifaceted relationship. Sexuality was a part of the larger whole, blessed and regulated by the community, because the community needed the family, and the family needed the community.

Now couples may no longer look to the community to provide economic and social support and sanctions. What they may fail to realize is that our most profound human capability to be intimate with others and to be fruitful within our community is being crippled by a culture that converts our sexual nature into a consumer product. Couples may long for a deeper understanding of sexuality but discover that their church is afraid to speak about sexuality's power. They may wish for community support but worry that their sexual desires are not understood. They may even wish they could counter the domination of the wedding industry but do not know where to start.

Can weddings become public events that engage the community and the couple in ways that reorient sexuality toward a full-orbed practice of marriage? Can our weddings become celebratory events that establish honest marriage relationships? Can weddings speak about sexual intimacy as a gift of God that nonetheless requires an investment of attention and effort? Can we recognize sex as a gift we will not fully enjoy if community support and encouragement are absent?

The transition from singleness into marriage is not an easy one, despite our romantic notions. We need marriage rituals that acknowledge the difficulties, admitting that sexual intimacy in its fullest sense does not come easily within our society of consumerism. But above all, couples need to know that God delights in marriages in which sexual intimacy mirrors the love that God has for the church and for humankind. The church must focus its wedding preparation and wedding services on celebrating this kind of love. Then what we say and celebrate in weddings will be good news for the dancers and for the church.

Images of Intimacy
Reflection 15: October 8, 2016

Romans 12:9-10

Gary: It has been our delight to watch the budding and growing of your relationship, Astrid and Armin, and it is now our delight to participate in your wedding.

Lydia: Armin and Astrid, you have chosen a wonderful text for your wedding service. Romans 12 is rich in insight, challenge, and wisdom. This text really comes out of the long "wisdom" tradition of the Bible. One way to think of this wisdom is to see it as a recipe – a recipe for building a healthy relationship and a healthy community. Surely, Paul directs these nuggets of wisdom to the whole church, but they certainly also apply to growing an intimate relationship.

Gary: A month ago, the congregation held a shower for you that included not only a larger gift but also a more personal element – you were gifted with some favourite recipes from your faith community. There is something very symbolic about that. For your marriage "recipe collection," you need to bring together the best insights, experiences, and wisdom from your family systems, from your faith community, but also from your broader work and friendship networks.

Lydia: Paul is very insightful here in Romans 12. He offers some wonderful ingredients to put into your collection. We want to highlight five of these. Just one word of caution! As any good cook knows, it takes more than just getting the right ingredients together to make a good bread or casserole. There is also an art involved – a sense of timing, of experimenting, of tasting, of flexibility, of improvising, of adjusting something here and there. The small picture is the list of ingredients. The large picture is how they all fit together. We start with the small picture – the list of ingredients.

Gary: #1: Vulnerability and honesty. "Let love be genuine; hate what is evil, hold fast to what is good." Let love be genuine. Love grows out of the deepest part of who you are. There can be no pretending. No falsehood. No hiding your true self from the other. It takes a huge amount of vulnerability to expose the deepest part of who you are to your beloved. A bit later, Paul adds, "Do not claim to be wiser than you are." Don't pretend with each other. Be honest with each other. Be vulnerable with each other. This ingredient needs to be injected into every aspect of your lives together in order to be effective if you want your intimacy level to keep rising!

Lydia: #2: Mutuality. "Love one another with mutual affection; outdo each other in showing honour." And then, a bit later, Paul adds, "Live in harmony with one another." Mutuality and harmony. Ah, this is kind of a marriage-long journey. Role definitions and expectations between spouses have been changing dramatically. No one now is expecting to be head of the household because of gender. Role definitions are open and flexible. But they do need to be talked about and mutually agreed upon. Like when Gary and I preserve dill pickles together (I used to do this all by myself). We each know what our job is. It is a fully mutual undertaking. It is efficient and fast – and enjoyable.

Yet we also have a certain division of labour – for example, Gary bakes bread, and I bake *Zwieback*. I know you have already experimented with cooking together and know that it works best if each of you brings your best skill to the task and then mutually work out when to lead and when to follow the other's leading.

Gary: #3: Passion. "Do not lag in zeal, be ardent in spirit, serve the Lord. Rejoice in hope, be patient in suffering." Passionate words, these. Don't be afraid to be passionate – of being open emotionally, of celebrating with each other, of crying together, of being passionate in lovemaking, of living your marriage with emotional freedom. (I experienced a lot of emotional reserve when we were first married. I wanted to control my deeper emotions. This was not healthy for our marriage. I needed to be set free from emotional over-control.) Passion adds the necessary spice to the marriage, something invaluable in a gourmet relationship.

Lydia: #4: Prayer. "Serve the Lord...persevere in prayer." The marriage story you are creating and growing, Astrid and Armin, is one you want to live in the context of God's love for you. It is a sacred story. It is a story that includes worship and prayer – both as a part of a faith community but also in your story as a couple. It is always a challenge for a couple to nurture their spiritual lives as individuals and as a couple. Praying is a part of that. Praying is a very intimate and vulnerable part of a marriage that is lived within God's story. Personal prayer. Couple prayer. Community prayer. No wonder Jesus taught his followers to pray, knowing they desired the intimacy with God which Jesus exhibited. Persevere in prayer.

Gary: #5: Hospitality and service. "Contribute to the needs of the saints: extend hospitality to strangers." We delight in the commitment that both of you have to service and hospitality. Armin, you have been involved in Mennonite Disaster Service, and I know both of you are committed to continuing this kind of hands-on involvement in responding to the needs of others. Service and hospitality, I think, are part of your DNA and part of your larger family's DNA. Both sets of grandparents and parents have modelled these in wonderful ways. Continue to live out this story and this challenge from Paul. "Contribute to the needs of the saints: extend hospitality to strangers." Hospitality and service push you beyond your small family circle and into what God is doing in the world.

Lydia: We have looked at five ingredients Paul offers, which we think offer promise for a healthy marriage relationship. We have the ingredients for this recipe before us – vulnerability and honesty, mutuality, passion, prayer, hospitality, and service. In one sense, this is still the small picture listing of individual pieces of a good relationship. Ingredients alone, however, are never enough. How do these now fit together into the larger picture of a tasty and healthy marriage diet?

Gary: Who are the cooks, the bakers, the ones who will put these ingredients together? The cooks are two very unique human beings, each with a whole set of strengths and weaknesses. Like each of us here, Armin and Astrid, you, we are sure, will know success and failure, joy and pain, laughter and sorrow, special moments in the midst of lots of routine, exhilaration and depression – maybe even despair. You need to accept and acknowledge your humanness. Sometimes the cake just flops – it just doesn't rise enough – but you eat it anyway.

But there is a bigger picture here.

Lydia: The bigger picture starts with knowing that in your humanness, you are still deeply loved. The central claim of our faith is that God loves us unconditionally – loves us as human as we are, despite our faults and our failures. And knowing your two families as well as we do, we know that you grew up in the context of deep, unconditional love. Being loved gives you self-worth. You don't have to earn your worth by baking a perfect marriage cake.

Gary: Knowing that you are deeply, unconditionally loved – by God and by your families, and now by your spouse, you are set free to love unconditionally in return, to be vulnerable to each other, to fully explore the many facets of intimacy, to allow the complex and many-sided spectrum of emotions and feeling space in your relationship.

Lydia: Two months ago, Gary and I celebrated 52 years of marriage. And we did feel like celebrating. We have had difficult moments in our relationship. We have had conflicts. We have not always understood each other. Once, we were close to crisis. But in the end, we know that we love deeply and are deeply loved. And that makes all the difference.

Gary: We do celebrate an intimate relationship. Intimacy is always a bit mysterious. So often, it comes in ways that surprise us. It comes as a gift. It comes in unexpected moments. But it comes, we think, within the big picture of an intimate relationship that grows out of knowing we are loved by God and by the other.

Lydia: Astrid and Armin, as we celebrate this day with you, we pray that your relationship with each other will keep on growing and deepening and becoming more and more intimate. You have the recipe before you. You are on your way to becoming master chefs.

Gary & Lydia: Blessings and joy on your marriage journey as you set the table of your relationship with vulnerability, honesty, mutuality, passion, prayer, and hospitality. From that space, you will radiate welcome and joy to your larger family, to friends, to your community, and to strangers you will meet along the way.

An Encompassing Intimacy
Reflection 16: November 24, 2007

1 Corinthians 13:4-6

The Search for Intimacy

We are all on a lifelong quest for closeness, for love, for intimacy. That is our deepest human need. Hopefully, we experience a childhood intimacy with our parents. Hopefully, we experience unconditional love, a closeness and security that gives us a deep sense of self-worth and gives us the freedom to develop other intimate relationships. But, not all parents are able to meet this universal need of their children. Hopefully, we experience some levels of intimacy with our larger family circles and with good friends, and with our primary communities – perhaps the church or professional community.

But marriage is where our hopes and longings for intimacy are the greatest, the deepest, the most idealized. But marriage is a complex relationship, and intimacy a complicated concept, and not all marriages meet our hopes and longings.

Today, "Ruth" and "Bill," I celebrate both the richness and the complexity of a wedding and a marriage that seeks to bring together persons of different religious backgrounds and different cultures. It brings together two people who love each other in a permanently committed way. You faced many complexities in your relationship already, the crossing of religious and cultural traditions not the only ones. Even your geographical distance from each other at times has been a challenge for you. But you have discovered some very deep gifts in each other, and a bonding that gives you confidence in your relationship; a bonding perhaps strengthened by these challenges.

Every marriage relationship is a very complex thing, as Lydia and I have certainly experienced in our 43 years of living together. One of the challenges of every marriage is how to keep on growing an intimate relationship that embraces every aspect of who we are, an intimacy that is all-encompassing. For people of faith, a core intimacy is spiritual. And that, as we have explored rather deeply the last few months in our time of marriage preparation, will be one of your complex challenges. How can two people from different faith backgrounds find, develop, and live out a spiritual intimacy? It won't be enough to just tolerate each other's religious peculiarity, to sort of live and let live in the religious sphere. That won't be enough for the two of you.

I want to offer a few reflections on an intimate relationship generally and then on spiritual intimacy particularly.

The Meaning of Intimacy

What do we mean by intimacy? It is very hard to define. But I would start with words and phrases like "closeness," or "deep connections with another person," or "feeling at one with another," or "engaging each other at deep levels." We could talk about "looking into each other's very being," or of "touching another at the core of who that person is," or of "moments when you feel at one with another person." Intimacy is a many-faceted, mysterious, compelling, wonderful thing. But it is also very elusive. You can't capture it. You can't program it. You can't guarantee it. It wants to slip away from us. And yet, when it happens, nothing in the world is better. Certainly, intimacy is something much bigger than only sexual intercourse.

The Scope of Intimacy

What is intimacy's scope? Our society has tended to make the meaning of intimacy a very shallow thing. For many people, intimacy means sex. Period. You are intimate when you are making love. But physical intimacy is only one part of a much bigger whole, a whole which encompasses our entire being:

- **emotional intimacy**, this includes feeling level connections and sharing. It includes being open to all the emotional colourings and experiences of the other. It includes being in tune with each other's joy and pain and anger, ecstasy and dreams and loss of dreams, and good moments and bad moments. It is being emotionally vulnerable with each other.
- **intellectual intimacy**. Discussing ideas. Challenging each other's thinking. Sharing your reading and your insights with each other. Probably, because of your common education and professions, this kind of intimacy will be easy and natural for you.
- **social intimacy**. Having a shared network of

friends. Developing a mutually satisfying
community. Entertaining people. Going out
together into the public sphere.

- **recreational intimacy.** Enjoying going
  together to a movie, a concert, a sports event,
  camping, or playing tennis...
- **physical, sexual intimacy.** Enjoying each
  other's bodies. When all the other intimacies are in
  place, the physical intimacy can grow and deepen
  through the whole lifetime of your marriage.
  (During the last few months, Lydia and I have been
  reading through the "Wisdom literature" in the
  Bible together. This week, we finished reading the
  "Song of Solomon." What a marvellous, sensual,
  erotic book. And yet, Christians have often been
  very uncomfortable with it and mostly either
  neglect it or try to "spiritualize" it. It is a great book
  for husband and wife to read together.)
- **and then, finally, is spiritual intimacy** –
  together looking beyond yourselves to a higher
  power. (see Appendix, 'Flower of Intimacy
  Exercise')

Together, being open to the transcendent and the mysterious. Together, looking for deeper meaning in your lives. And
this is where you two, people of different religious traditions,
will have particular challenges – and perhaps opportunities.
Can you, without giving up your own identity and convictions
and without just going your own independent spiritual ways,
find ways to grow spiritually together? We began to explore
some of these dimensions in our time together.

One way was to talk about your respective traditions a lot,
to share these with each other, and to discuss them intellectu-

ally. Keep on naming to each other what out of your respective traditions is important to you. Be ready to ask the other about their traditions, deeper meanings, and symbols.

But talking won't be enough. You will also need to "do" spiritual things together. For example, learn each other's hymns and sing them together. Or develop common rituals and prayers, even developing a sacred space in your home where you can share the symbols of each of your faiths. Or go on retreats together where you are both nurtured – perhaps in a nature setting. Go to each other's places of community worship.

You also talked about "serving together." Serving others is a core value of each of your traditions. Find causes, or places, or needs that you can address together.

To me, spiritual intimacy, reaching out to God – both alone and together – suggests an openness to change, to grow, to be open to something that is bigger and more encompassing than anything we know now. Who knows where that will yet take you?

An Image

I want to leave you with a final image. I want you to look at each other's hands. One of yours is white, the other brown. You can communicate a great deal to the other with your hands. You can have your hands open to the other, welcoming, inviting, opening yourself to the other. Or you can turn your hand over, saying with that, "stay away, don't come too close, give me space." You can even close your hand in a fist to the other, a hostile, aggressive – or defensive mode.

And you can hold each other's hands – a thing of closeness, of companionship, of love, of intimacy. It is a beautiful thing, isn't it? A white hand and a brown hand, held in an embrace.

But you can't be holding hands with each other all the time. As Gibran said, "Love one another, but make not a bond of love... Sing and dance and be joyous, but let each of you be alone."[1] There is a rhythm to this intimacy thing, a rhythm of being together and being apart, of closeness and distance, of holding hands and of keeping your hands to yourself. You want to continue to be self-differentiated and not enmeshed, intimate but not fused, together but not submerged in the other. Neither of you can dare lose the true colour of your hand or the true colour of your identity and being.

There is one more hand position that is important to me. That is the hand reaching out to God to embrace the loving hand of God reaching out to us. Whether the symbol is hands folded in prayer or lifted above your head in praise or reaching to touch some symbol of the sacred, it is your hands that can symbolize the embrace of love for God and the love of God.

May you, "Ruth" and "Bill," know a very genuine intimate marriage relationship. May you, as individuals and as a couple, know the intimate love of God.

> Love is patient; love is kind; love is not envious or boastful or arrogant or rude. It does not insist on its own way... It bears all things, believes all things, hopes all things, endures all things.
>
> 1 Corinthians 13:4-6, NRSV

Love is the greatest of all gifts.
Amen.

Love in a Reflective Mode
Reflection 17: July 2, 1989

Celebrating 25 Years of Being Married

Ephesians 3:14-19

As some of you already know, Lydia and I are about to celebrate 25 years of being married to each other. In the great scheme of things, this event is surely very insignificant, though for us two, it has some importance. The fact that we want to celebrate the event, to mark it by gathering friends together, is our way of thanking God for an abundance of love which God has directed our way.

Today, I would like to do some reflecting on the growth of a marriage. I will not do justice to our summer theme, "finding God in the city." That theme will come up only very indirectly, though perhaps I could call this meditation "on growing a relationship on urban soil." After all, two farmer types ended up spending their entire married life in the city.

Several weeks ago, friends from Edmonton, where I had been a pastor for 15 years, dropped in. In giving their regrets for coming a month early for our celebration, they reminisced about their own silver wedding some five years ago. They reflected on the pastoral visit I had with them at that time. Then, they asked me a pointed question. "Who is pastor to you? Who helps you reflect on the course of your marriage? Who asks you the kind of questions which can help give insight into your relationship? We valued your coming to us as pastor at that point in our lives. Who pastors you?"

The saying, "the person who tries to self-doctor has a fool for a patient" applies equally to one who tries to "self-pastor." I confess that this sermon is an attempt at "self-pastoring," an attempt at being self-reflective about being married for 25 years. I do this publicly, also probably a foolish thing to do, on the assumption that there is something universal about the joys and stresses of a marriage relationship. And I do it publicly because both thanksgiving and confession belong within the faith community, and both are good for the soul, they say.

I remember asking this couple to use the image of a journey to help them reflect on their marriage. How did the journey begin? What were the high points and low points of the journey? Where were the bumps and potholes? Were there some detours or construction signs which indicated some repair work needed to be done? Where have been the yield signs where you became aware you needed to yield to each other? What have you used as a roadmap? What is your destination, and how are you planning to get there? What impact has your faith had on your relationship journey?

In a general way, I want to follow these self-administered questions in my reflections this morning. I want to use a text from Ephesians as one of the road signs for our journey.

"For this reason I bow my knees before the Father, from whom every family in heaven and on earth takes its name. I pray that, according to the riches of his glory, he may grant that you may be strengthened in your inner being with power through his Spirit, and that Christ may dwell in your hearts through faith, as you are being rooted and grounded in love. I pray that you may have the power to comprehend, with all the saints, what is the breadth and length and height and depth, and to know the love of Christ that surpasses knowledge, so that you may be filled with all the fullness of God." (Eph 3:14-19, NRSV)

I will obviously take this passage out of context and apply it both to our relationship with God and to the relationship between husband and wife. The images that grab me are – the width, length, height, and depth of love. I am intrigued that Paul says we can know this love though it surpasses knowledge.

But first, the story. Ah, the mysteries of love. Ah, the naivete of a farmer very inexperienced in the ways of women. I, after all, had no sisters. And I had been far too timid to seriously date anyone in high school. Yes, I had a terrific, wonderful crush on a girl in grade 8. But it only made me miserable since I was far too shy to let her know about it. She was blissfully and happily unaware of my racing heart when she went by. I did date a few times in high school, and even though I liked one girl quite a lot, I remained totally inexperienced in the ways of women – and of romantic love.

On to CMBC. I blush even now to recall it. Shatteringly unromantic it was. Several of us first-year fellows thought it would be nice to go on a date, but since we didn't know any of the girls yet, we went down the student list and, in lottery fashion, chose someone to call. I vaguely remembered that a certain Lydia Neufeld had been playing ping pong in the gym a few days earlier. Not a bad player – for a girl. Why not call her? That first date showed no promise at all for a continuing relationship. A double date it was, off to watch a football game with my beloved Calgary Stampeders playing the Winnipeg Blue

Bombers. I didn't talk. I watched football. The other couple talked and were fun to be with. My date didn't even like football. She envied the other girl's luck of the draw. They, by the way, also got married to each other.

Our relationship took three years to grow into some semblance of committed love. It could not have been predicted. A few dates here and there, dating others, some flickering of interest, and then a long parting of ways. I had some serious growing up to do. We were a most unlikely match, a fact underlined when we first met each other's families. We were seeing each other again, seriously enough now for Lydia to invite me to her home in Niagara for Christmas.

What a shock for an introvert from a thoroughly introverted family. I teased the Neufelds long afterwards that they were all so busy talking when we arrived that it took me till the next day to find an opening to say hello. And after we were married, it could be said that there was real purpose in my being a part of the Neufeld family. Since they were always all talking, there had to be someone around who would listen.

Now, of course, Lydia could tell her own stories of meeting the Harders. There, it seemed everyone was into listening and no one into talking much. She also had a major contribution to make to the Harders.

And we soon realized that family patterns play an important role in one's marriage ideals and in the expectations one has of each other. Peace and quiet were my recipe for an ideal home life. Noise and activity were Lydia's prescription. We are still working on sorting this one out.

A week after we announced our engagement, there came a huge crisis in my life. My dad had another heart attack, and the doctor said he might not survive. Lydia and I sought the prayer room at CMBC. Something very important happened there in that prayer room. No, Dad did not get healed. He did die a few days later. I did get home in time to be with my family as we held vigil with Dad as he passed into eternity. But in that prayer room, I found a stillness and calmness to face the pain ahead. And Lydia and I knew that we could pray together. We knew that at the most basic level of our beings, evidenced in crisis, we shared faith together, and we could seek God together. And that has been significant for us through the past 25 years.

We build praying together into the pattern of our lives. Of course, our prayers are often only routine, a going through the motions. But we say very consciously that we want to bring our lives, the routine and the more eventful, before God each day. And that nourishes us. And sometimes, especially around crisis, or around the coming into our lives of a child, or around major decision making, praying together has been a profound experience of intimacy, perhaps more intimate even than sexual intercourse.

We were married in 1964 at a time when there was a very mixed family agenda. My family was still grieving the death of my father some three months earlier. Mom had an almost over-whelming mixture of emotions to deal with. Yet she fully encouraged us and, by the wedding day, was genuinely happy for us.

Over the years, we realized how much our marriage has been shaped and influenced by our families – how much the modeling of our parents affected us.

Lydia's family was so much more vocal about everything. They expressed their thoughts and their feelings so much more freely than did the Harders. They loved a rip-roaring argu-ment. Lydia and her dad could argue to the point of both shouts and tears, and when it was over with, there were no carry-over feelings. Their love was never threatened by their disagreements. I had so much to learn about expressing my feelings, about not bottling things up inside where you can't deal with them.

My parents expressed their love and their faith in quieter ways. Their love for each other was obvious, even though they were not openly affectionate with each other. And always, there was so much respect and appreciation for each other.

And they modelled to me that you can make changes in your relationship mid-stream. It happened on a Sunday morning. Dad tended toward impatience. He did the chores early, ate breakfast, and perhaps went over the choir music that he would conduct that day in church. He was always one to get to church 20 minutes early. Mom had more to get ready on a Sunday morning, getting kids in shape for church, doing household chores, preparing dinner for company almost every Sunday, and getting herself ready. This Sunday, Dad was particularly impatient. And Mom wasn't ready when Dad was. He said, "*schpoud de* (hurry up), you're always late." Mom responded, "If you want me to get ready in time you can help me. Otherwise go to church by yourself and I'll stay home."

And always, after that exchange, Dad helped Mom on a Sunday morning, and they got ready for church together. I marvelled that conflict could lead to change and to greater happiness. That continues to give me hope.

But back to our marriage. We got married without the benefit of pre-marriage counselling, of helpful books to read, of help in understanding the dynamics of an intimate relationship. And it showed. I was, at 22 years of age, probably too young for marriage – too naïve, too unaware of what was happening inside of me. But I was confident and in love. We didn't have a very good first year of marriage. I was a final year student at CMBC, fully into student life, president of the student body, having one important meeting after another. Lydia taught a very difficult class in school. And we didn't really know how to connect with each other about what was happening to us. I was totally into traditional marriage roles. Lydia, not so much so. We needed help and didn't have the sense to ask for it. This stupid male was almost blissfully unaware of how poorly we were communicating about the important things we were experiencing.

But we were so much in love. Yet, what does love look like when you are 23 years old and have a tender marriage plant which needs nurturing and tending and watering and maybe pruning, but you are too self-absorbed to pay attention to any of these?

Maybe it was by the grace of God that love grew despite us, and the plant became sturdier, and the thing survived and even flourished. The next years were "exciting." We grew together.

I experienced the call to ministry, which Lydia fully supported. She continued to teach. We moved to Sudbury. Mark was born. We moved to Goshen/Elkhart for further education. We studied together. Kendall was born. There is nothing more profoundly "intimate" than to hold a newborn baby in arms, minutes old, and to offer a prayer of thanksgiving and dedication together.

In our eighth year of marriage, very suddenly, our relationship was in crisis. This time, the shaking of the foundations was much more threatening than it was that first year. Then we were mostly unaware of our stumbling. Now, we became painfully aware that something was wrong.

I was taking a year of internship training in London, Ontario, a part of my seminary program to prepare myself better for pastoral ministry. It was an exciting year for me. I was being supervised. I was in a small encounter group. For really the first time, I was becoming aware of some of my inner emotional dynamics. That year brought all kinds of challenging experiences, stimulation, a probing of my insides, and feedback on how I was doing in ministry. And I would come home in the evening so emotionally drained, though happy, that I had no energy left to give to my marriage relationship. I would shut Lydia and the kids out and vegetate behind the newspaper or in front of the TV.

Lydia, meanwhile, was at home in a small basement apartment dealing with two small children and with intense feelings of aloneness and of being shut out of my exciting world. We were growing apart very quickly. And soon we knew we were in a marriage crisis and that unless we did something about it, we would continue to grow apart, and there wouldn't be much left of our relationship.

We knew we needed help. We asked for it and got it (an intense small couple's group led by a psychiatrist, sessions with a clinical supervisor), and started growing together again. Our marriage plant dug deeper roots that year through crisis and pain and set the stage for a more joyful flourishing.

One of the joys of our relationship over the years has been our common love of theology. At its beginnings, we studied Greek together at CMBC, though it always mystified me that we could study the same stuff at the same time and Lydia always got the better grades. Maybe I wasn't paying full attention to the Greek.

Many a sermon has been forged in the debate over a theological point of view or a biblical text – or an analysis of our contemporary world's challenges. A few months ago, I wasn't getting under the skin of a particular text. We drove to Niagara to visit Lydia's mother and spent the entire trip arguing vigorously and even heatedly over its interpretation. At the end, I found a new understanding which went beyond both of ours and I like to think that the sermon was much richer for it. We have valued, enjoyed, and cherished our common interest in theology – and our ease in arguing things out.

The journey continues. More highs and lows, bumps and detour signs are inevitable. But I look forward to the road ahead. Our marriage has more growing to do yet. We expect God to continue to provide fuel for the journey and love for the relationship. We haven't yet fully grasped how wide and long and high and deep the love of Christ is, nor the full potential of our own love for each other.

The passage from Ephesians still makes an emotional impact on me when I read it. "For this reason I bow my knees before the Father, from whom every family in heaven and on earth takes its name" (Eph 3:14, NRSV).

Our family, my family, gets its name from God. We are in God's care. God knows us, and names us, and calls us God's children. "I pray that, according to the riches of his glory, he may grant that you may be strengthened in your inner being with power through his Spirit, and that Christ may dwell in your hearts through faith" (Eph 3:16-17, NRSV). I feel very strongly that our marriage has been a gift from God, that its growing and loving has been nourished by God's glorious riches. I shudder to think what our relationship would look like now without God's sustaining presence, without our common faith, without the values that come from our faith, and without a community of God's people to help us understand the deeper dimensions of love. My spirit is filled with thanksgiving.

"I pray that you may have the power to comprehend, with all the saints, what is the breadth and length and height and depth, and to know the love of Christ that surpasses knowledge" (Eph 3:18-19, NRSV). Surely these words are directed to us so that we become more fully aware of God's love for us. We marvel more and more at the incredible love of Christ. We become more and more aware of all of its dimensions – its all-encompassing width and length and height and depth.

And then Paul ends that sentence by saying that we can

know that love, even though it surpasses knowledge. There is a knowing that goes beyond knowledge. There is a knowing of God which can go beyond what our mind can grasp of God. There is a knowing of another person which goes beyond communication skills and descriptions.

There is a magnificent Hebrew word יָדַה which has been translated as "to know." It is the word "*yadah.*" It is a wonderful word. *Yadah* is used in the Bible to talk about how we can know and love God, to know God personally and intimately. It is used to describe how God knows and loves us. When the Psalmist says that God knows us even before we are born – knows our inmost thoughts and desires and hopes and pains – the word used is "*Yadah.*"

That same word – *yadah* – is also used in the Old Testament for sexual intercourse. And he 'knew' his wife, and she conceived and bore Cain (Gen 4:1). Sexual intercourse is thus assumed to be an expression of a deep knowing of another person. It is assumed that there is a profound personal, emotional, and spiritual intimacy present that surrounds the physical intimacy. The physical and emotional come together at a depth level. I believe that such a "knowing," which brings together emotional and physical intimacy, is possible only in a committed relationship, a relationship in which two persons are totally committed to each other. Then, the knowing of each other has a height and depth and width and breadth to it because it is a knowing of love and in love. Then, the word *yadah* can be a beautiful description of sexual intercourse.

Just think of it. The same word – *yadah* – is used both to describe God "knowing" us and to describe us "knowing" another through sexual intercourse. *Yadah* expresses an intimate knowing, maybe a knowing that surpasses knowledge.

Back to our own story, and to Lydia and I wanting to celebrate 25 years of marriage. We stumble along enough in our marriage to realize that we have not yet, in the words of Paul, been "filled with all the fullness of God" (Eph 3:19, NRSV). But then, we aren't finished with our journey yet. The passage from Ephesians is both a road map for the future and a promise of God's love, which will sustain and nurture our marriage.

There has been enough joy and love though, that we are overwhelmingly grateful to God and feel like celebrating. And we want to tell everyone that we love each other. You are all invited to come and join the celebration with us!

A Prayer of Thanks and Confession

*God, Creator, giver of life, ultimate source of love and
loving, we give thanks for how you created us – sexual
beings, relational beings, loving beings – an awesome
awareness that we are wonderfully made – made in your
very image. We give thanks, Creator God, for the beautiful gift of our sexuality, with all its beauty, power,
mystery, complexity, and challenges. We celebrate our
sexuality in all its complicated beauty. We celebrate
healthy sexual relationships. We celebrate the sexuality
of persons who choose to live out who they are as single
persons in community with many friends. We delight in
the sheer beauty and power and joy of being sexual
beings. We give thanks for the many biblical stories, the
poetry and wisdom, that help us ponder the delights and
complexities, and temptations and abuses of our human
sexual story. We also acknowledge and confess that in
our humanness, we are tempted to use our sexuality in
hurtful, abusive, and selfish ways. Adam and Eve's story
is also our story. We acknowledge that Eden is no more.
And yet – and yet – you offer us forgiveness, healing,
loving and joy, and delight in how you created us.
We pray for healing for all who have been abused and
wounded. We pray for all who abuse their personal
power and violate their partner's trust. We pray for
healing of broken relationships. We pray that the church
can become a community that both confronts abuse, and
offers a vision for how we can live out God's wonderful
gift of sexuality. We pray in the name of Jesus, the
confronter and the healer. Amen.*

Part Five

Appendix: Resources

Appendix 1: Flower of Intimacy Exercise

The leader discusses the various facets of intimacy in a relationship with the couple. Each partner then fills out their own answers to the following questions as an exercise to be done at home. Then they share their answers with each other and discuss the direction in which they want to grow. At the next session, the leader asks them what insights they gained from their conversation.

Which petals represent the strength of your relationship?
Which petals do you particularly need to work to develop?
Which petals represent the vision of intimacy you each hold?
Which petal have you neglected thus far?
Which petal is not important to you?

2. An Essay on Homosexuality

A Biblical & Pastoral Perspective, Presented at Pastoral Event, Fall 2003

I have been asked to share with you colleagues something of my journey in reading the Scriptures on the topic of homosexuality. On the one hand, I am pleased to do so. It has forced me to look closely at many texts again, and I do want to be held accountable by you for my reading of the Scriptures. On the other hand, I am reluctant to do so, mostly because I am not a biblical scholar and don't have the necessary tools to do a thorough reading, but also because it seems like the church can't deal with this controversial topic without people getting wounded. Neither am I an academic theologian. My world and work do not start with broad philosophical frameworks nor detailed analysis of words (that is, with the academy) but with people and their relationships and the meaning that faith and the Scriptures give them (that is, the Church).

From here, I make observations and raise questions which I think do have a broader impact but whose systematic formulations are beyond my abilities. For this paper I am borrowing from a pastoral letter I wrote to our congregation last April in which I tried to explain my personal views and convictions regarding human sexuality.

I must acknowledge up front that I am, of course, not objective nor neutral in how I read the Bible or think about homosexuality. I do not think it is possible for anyone to be. I will try to name my biases, for I'm sure they will show anyway. No interpretation of Scripture is ever purely objective and value free. I am more on the "open" and "including" side of the debate. Articles I have published and comments I have made publicly over a number of years would indicate this.

I very much appreciated the very rigorous study our congregation undertook over the last year and a half and the large number of very knowledgeable and gifted people from within our congregation who led various aspects of this study. I have valued the opportunity to struggle with this very complex issue and to clarify for myself what my understandings and convictions are. I have especially appreciated the rigorous Bible studies. In some ways, it has been a difficult time for me, especially as I am aware of the diversity of convictions, strongly held, in our congregation. It has also been difficult for me as pastor because, despite our best intentions and planning, we did hurt each other in the end, and a huge healing and reconciliation task confronts us. But it has also been a good time for me, rich in learning and rich in the challenge of trying to sort out what it means to be a pastor involved in a complex process around an issue the church is deeply divided over.

Foundational Convictions

I will first state some of my foundational convictions, which frame any process of dialogue around any controversial topic for a church body that takes faith and the Scriptures seriously.

1) We are committed to Jesus Christ. Our discussion and

discernment is taking place within a church context, that is, within a context of a Christian community of faith. The essence of this community is a commitment to Jesus Christ as Saviour and Lord. This includes my/our commitment to try our best to follow Jesus and his way in life. In my opinion, I am ready to worship with, fellowship with, and dialogue with anyone and everyone who makes this commitment to Christ. I support our present congregational practice (TUMC) of requiring only a confession of faith in Jesus Christ as a criterion for church membership.

2) We are a "People of the Book." To me, this means a commitment to the Holy Scriptures as an authoritative guide to faith and to how we should live our lives. The Bible is identity shaping for us as a Christian people. I experience it constantly as a powerful life-giving and freeing Word of God. I think that we have taken the Scriptures very, very seriously in our process. I am committed to a serious wrestling with the Scriptures. I am fully aware that within our congregation and within our conference people have different starting places in terms of how they read the Scriptures and which Scriptures they find foundational for this discussion. I am fully aware of differing interpretations and understandings of these Scriptures among us. We do bring different experiences and questions to the Scriptures and thus read and interpret them differently. But we are a people of the Word. Whether we come out on the more "closed" side or the more "open" side of our discernment, we need to be very rigorous in our biblical work. And we need to be respectful of people who read the Scriptures differently than we do and thus come out with different convictions. It is clear to me that on the issue of homosexuality, both sides of the debate have very deeply held Gospel convictions.

3) We are a Mennonite church. This presupposes a commitment to the Body of Christ, the Church, including the

universal church, the Mennonite peoplehood, and our local congregations. I/we do need to be accountable to the wider church and to its statements and confessions of faith. I very much affirm the new *Confession of Faith in a Mennonite Perspective* (1995). I voted for it in St. Louis. But to me, it does not have the status of a "creed." It is not Holy Scripture. It is a human document which will continue to evolve and change as the Spirit of God continually works in our midst. To me, it is significant how much change there already has been in this confession from our last one on the topic of human sexuality and family.

4) The Holy Spirit continues to work in our world and in our church. Being Christian means making a commitment to being led by the Spirit of God. I believe the Spirit of God is acting and wants to lead the Church in meeting the challenges of every new day, including our day. Because we humans, including Christian humans, cannot ever fully understand God, and God's revelation, and God's will for us, God's Spirit continues the work of revealing these to us. It may be that in understanding homosexuality — honouring the dignity and personhood of all no matter how they name themselves — God's active Spirit will shed new light to guide our journey.

5) We are sexual beings who are followers of Jesus. To me, this means that we make a commitment to being Christian in the way we live our lives as sexual beings. I believe there is a Christian/biblical sexual ethic for each of us who name ourselves followers of Christ. We are invited and challenged to discover what it means for us to be followers of Christ in the way we live out and express our sexual selves.

I think most of us share most of these common commitments. If we do, then we have a very strong basis on which to continue struggling together in discernment over our understandings of homosexuality. The above convictions also mean that I do not self-identify myself (or TUMC, for that matter) as "liberal," at least not in how "liberal" is popularly understood as just an easy, tolerant acceptance of anything and everything. I self-identify myself as evangelical (not necessarily in the sense of "evangelical theology," but in its biblical sense), Gospel-centered, Christ-centered, biblical, missional, Anabaptist/Mennonite, and needing empowering by the Holy Spirit. I see my/our identity much more as "traditional" (preaching and teaching the basic traditions of the Gospel), with confidence in the "foundational" Scriptures and in worship.

Presuppositions (biases)

I also want to acknowledge some of my presuppositions or biases. These, I hope, reflect more than either prejudice or political correctness, but rather grow out of my work and study as a Christian and as a pastor.

1) I value diversity, difference, and healthy dialogue. (After all, I have lived an entire marriage with the richness of constant discussion, debate, arguments, and disagreements over a whole stream of biblical interpretations and theological viewpoints.) I see the Scriptures themselves reflecting streams of conviction and story that aren't always in agreement. I value hearing differing interpretations and understandings of the Scriptures that offer new insight. That means that I am comfortable with and not overly stressed by our differences of opinion on the issue of homosexuality. I consider our expression of these differences healthy. I want to acknowledge, however, the particular pain of those who are impacted personally by the words that are used. I know that many people do not share this particular bias of mine and find difference and conflict very daunting and intimidating. I acknowledge that when it comes to conflict

itself, I am sometimes more comfortable in theory than in practice.

I know that many people do not share this particular bias of mine and find difference and conflict very daunting and intimidating. I acknowledge that when it comes to conflict itself, I am sometimes more comfortable theoretically than practically. I believe that conflict expressed and handled well can be healthy and growth-producing. I know that emotionally though, I sometimes hesitate to enter conflict. Sometimes, I try to avoid conflict when I shouldn't. I do think that it is in dealing with conflict with each other in the body of Christ that we most need to be committed to a loving and respectful way of facing each other and expressing ourselves.

2) I acknowledge above that on the issue of homosexuality, I am biased toward a more open and accepting perspective. Partly, this comes from my work as pastor and from hearing the stories of incredible pain that Christian persons who are homosexuals (and their families) feel because they have been excluded from church and sometimes from family circles. Often they express a deep longing for church and for acceptance in the body of Christ (particularly in the Mennonite Church). The pain and hurt caused by the church run very deep. We are dealing here with people committed to Christ who happen to be same-sex oriented. We are dealing with brothers and sisters in Christ.

But a pastor's "experiential soft heart" is not alone an adequate grounding for a position on such a controversial topic. The grounding has to be more biblical and theological. I do think that the biblical and theological arguments used to exclude homosexuals and to name homosexuality a sin are not as convincing to me as the traditional view would claim. We have learned, over the years and over many different issues, not to base all our biblical understandings on a few proof texts, especially when there are only a few texts on a topic. That is, we look more broadly for overall biblical perspectives and ways of understanding who God is and what God requires of us. I do have a deep respect for those convictions and positions, which, based on scriptural understandings, are more closed to an acceptance of homosexuality. This is the traditional reading and the traditional position of our conference. But that reading of Scripture does not fully convince me. Whereas I do have a deep respect for more closed positions which are based on understandings of Scripture, I do not sympathize with arguments based on ignorance of homosexuality or an unwillingness to dialogue with persons who are gay or lesbian.

3) We urgently need each other. We need all the divergent voices in the church as we continue to struggle with this issue. Every voice needs to be respected, heard, and listened to. Within these divergent voices, my hope would be that we will eventually find "a mediating position which allows the polarities of inclusion and exclusion somehow to be reconciled."[1] To me, it is essential that for our dialogue on this issue to have integrity, we need to hear the voices of those who are not heterosexual.

4) It is much healthier for persons in the church who are gay to be able to be open about their orientation rather than to be in the closet (much healthier for both the church and the gay person). But for them to be open, church has to be a "safe place" in which to be out of the closet. This kind of openness does not mean suspending convictions about homosexuality. But it does mean a loving, accepting, respectful dialogue between people who are heterosexual and people who are gay.

5) Just as I would expect all Christians in the church who are heterosexual to live their sexual lives in a Christian way, so I would expect all Christians in the church who are gay to live their sexual lives in a Christian way. What this Christian way is

may not be fully clear to either heterosexuals or homosexuals. I personally have quite a traditional view of Christian sexual ethics. I believe that complete genital sexual expression belongs only within a covenanted relationship.

6) Our Anabaptist theology would suggest that the local congregation needs to be the central place where discernment on difficult issues gets processed. We are part of a larger people-hood and part of larger conferences. I value this immensely and have given much of my adult life to participating in various levels of leadership at various levels of these conferences. I am fully committed to being an integral part of our wider conference structures. TUMC itself is a particularly conference-minded congregation. I think that there must be a "covenantal" kind of relationship between conference and congregation, where each takes the other very seriously and continues to dialogue with each other when there are difficult issues to face. The breaking of this covenant from either side is a very serious breach of the relationship.

But Mennonites are essentially non-hierarchical and largely congregational in polity. We must be aware of what the larger church thinks, must be responsive to its statements (e.g. The sexuality statement from Saskatoon '86 and the *Confession of Faith*, 1995), and must invite dialogue with conference leaders over the issues we are struggling with. But in the end, it is the local congregation which must be a primary "hermeneutical community" where decisions are made. It is within the local congregation that serious study of issues must take place. It is in the local congregation where change begins to happen and where change is expressed in concrete ways. This presupposition would also suggest that congregations must respect each other's discernments, especially when they reach different conclusions.

7) We need to be very open, direct, and frank in talking

about sexual issues in the church. I think that sexuality should be talked about from the pulpit during worship. I want our children to know that we can talk about sex in church and in worship so that they know that we are trying to bring our sexual understandings and our lives under the Lordship of Jesus Christ.

8) My present understanding is that our sexual orientation is given, not chosen. It is not something that anyone chooses. Our orientation rather is something that we discover. For some people, discovering that they are same sex oriented is a straightforward journey that is clear from a very early age. For others, it is a long, slow process of struggle and soul-searching before they can name who they are. For all of us, there tends to be struggle and confusion in coming to terms with our sexuality and learning to be responsible sexual beings. All of us who are Christian struggle to bring our sexuality under the Lordship of Christ. For persons with a minority sexual orientation, with a long history of rejection by the majority orientation, the journey to a healthy sexual identity may be particularly difficult.

I doubt that we can easily change our orientation even if we want to and try to. I understand that our sexual orientation can be placed somewhere on a continuum line from strong extremes to a more indefinite middle (bisexual). Perhaps persons closer to the middle can make some choices about who they are attracted to (and can be seen to be changing their orientation). But how can one account for the vagaries of who we fall in love with? It follows for me that we are not accountable for our orientation but only for how we live out our lives with the sexual orientation given to us.

There are always exceptions to the above, as the many anecdotal stories testify to. Scientific studies have not yet said the final word on either causation or possibility of change, and people can quote studies from all points of view. Some people give only slight weight to biology and great weight to environment in terms of causation. Some people are very optimistic about the possibilities of changing one's orientation. I remain very skeptical of these directions.

Taking the Bible Seriously: The Particular Challenges

1) The challenges for those of us who are more "open" on this issue.

There are large challenges ahead of us for all who take the Scriptures seriously while wrestling with a word from the Lord regarding homosexuality. There are particular challenges for those of us who read the Scriptures in a way that would be more open to including homosexuals in the church. It is clear that in those passages in which same-sex sexual expression is mentioned, it is always seen as an "abomination." When same-sex genital relations are mentioned, they are mentioned in prohibitive language. It is clear that nowhere does the bible affirm same-sex covenants. There is a silence in the Scriptures about "blessing same-sex covenants." It is a huge challenge to deal seriously with both the prohibition and the silence. I am not capable of meeting that challenge.

The majority of Christian tradition, and certainly of Mennonite tradition, has read the Bible as a condemnation of homosexual sex. It is always a challenge to read the Scriptures in a way that moves away from or beyond the tradition. It is also a particular challenge to be self-critical of our culture and to be aware of the cultural influences that might predispose us to an open stance. It is important that we analyze our modern Western culture (especially the sexual revolution) to recognize the enormous impact it has on our understanding of human

sexuality and generally on a greater acceptance of homosexuality.

2) The challenges for those of us who are more "closed" on
this issue.

It seems to me that there are also enormous challenges
confronting those of us who read these scriptural texts more
literally and embrace the condemnation of homosexual sex.
Cultural analysis is a two-edged sword. Of course, those of us
on the more open side need to be aware of how our position is
culturally influenced. But so do those whose position is more
closed. Mennonites have tended to set up a dualism in which it
seems that culture, or "world" (including the sexual revolution),
is almost all evil – and the church almost all good. I think that
there was both evil and good in the sexual revolution and that
there is both good and evil in "the world" (and in the church
too, for that matter). Along with much that is unhealthy, the
sexual revolution has brought us much that I value. I am very
grateful for birth control, for much fuller equality between
males and females, and for the openness with which we can
discuss sexuality.

The Scriptures themselves always reflect a cultural
context. God always reveals God's will within a historical
and cultural context. As I understand it, other cultures
outside of Israel, in the formative years of biblical faith, spoke
in similar ways, assuming that homosexual activity was
unclean and an abomination. There is nothing particularly
revelational or new or cutting edge in Israel's texts here. In
New Testament times, there were cultures (Roman and
Greek) where there were very unhealthy expressions of same-
sex intimacy that might have been the foil for what Paul says
in Romans 1. (I don't have the tools to do the analysis of the
cultural embeddedness of biblical texts. I think it would be
very helpful for someone to do a scholarly analysis of the

cultural placement of the biblical texts which refer to homo-sexual sex.)

In the second place, surely our "closed-ness" to homosexu-ality is as profoundly culturally shaped as is our "open-ness." Or do we really think that our huge emotional investment in this topic comes solely and purely from how we read the Bible? Don't most of us have a prior "revulsion" which then informs how we read the texts? Don't we have to admit that for many Christians, there is a cultural bias which colours their reading? It is often argued that we must take into consideration the strong opinions of Christians (especially Mennonites) of other cultures on this issue. I quite agree. But they too are culturally located. I personally would not want to be culturally bound to treat homosexuals in the way many cultures do. (A person from an African country came into my office a short while ago. He had been imprisoned and tortured because he was a homo-sexual and totally cast out by his family and clan.)

There is a challenge to place the "hot button" nature of this issue for many people over against the fact that there are so few texts that deal with it. Whether there are 5 or 6 or 7 texts that mention homosexual sex (depending on how one reads some of the Greek words), it is clear that the Bible pays scant attention to the topic. Isn't one of the rules of good Bible study to give weight to those topics most often dealt with in the Bible? Issues like money and poverty, for example. Why is it that we make so ultra important what the Bible itself doesn't? (Isn't there a hint of cultural location here?)

I am inclined to agree with what Hubert Schwartzentruber, who writes about issues of poverty and wealth in the Bible, "Perhaps making homosexuality such a hot-button issue is a version of straining out a little gnat so we can swallow the big economic camel without getting an upset stomach."[2]

The few mentions of same-sex sexual expression in the

Bible suggest that it wasn't something the biblical writers thought much about or struggled with. In other words, they basically accepted the cultural norms of their day. On many other issues, the Bible records a sense of struggle as a new "word from the Lord" challenges cultural presuppositions. For example, there is a genuine struggle to understand what the Lord's will is regarding war, women in leadership, slavery, and many other issues. One can find texts on both sides of these issues. There is a live ferment about which direction God is inviting his people to move toward. Cultural assumptions are uprooted. It is only in our day – yes, in our culture – that the cultural embeddedness of the Bible's, and our own, understanding of homosexuality is being acknowledged, and the struggle unleashed about how we understand God's mind regarding it. I think it is a challenge to those who read the prohibition texts as God's will for today to explain how they are more than cultural taboos.

There is a challenge to make the prohibition texts, few as they are, apply to a same-sex covenantal relationship. (We are talking here about Christians who are gay and want to commit themselves to each other in a faithful, permanent relationship.) The passages in the Bible do not seem to focus on homosexuality as such. There is no word on "orientation" or on a faithful relationship. There is word of violence and rape and abuse. It is a huge challenge to translate the particular context and words of these texts into a condemnation of a covenanted homosexual relationship.

There is a challenge in dealing with the silence of Jesus on this issue. Jesus just doesn't mention it, either positively or negatively. It is certainly possible, perhaps even likely, that he would have shared his culture's negative opinion – but for us Mennonites who cling so closely to the words of Jesus, this silence is a huge challenge.

It is a challenge to somehow prove that moving from these culturally located texts to a closed position on homosexuality isn't just "proof-texting." Even just limiting a Bible study to a few texts already has the feel of proof-texting, no matter which methods or tools of study you use.

It is a challenge to deal with these texts within the canonical awareness of the seeming movement of the Bible, especially the New Testament, in the direction of inclusion, breaking down barriers, and finding oneself in the same church with former enemies. Both Jesus and Paul constantly critique those who hold too closely to rules and who are legalists. Most of the New Testament seems to wage this battle. How is reading these texts more narrowly any different from being the kind of pharisee or scribe whom Jesus challenged so sharply?

It is a challenge to deal with the fact that we read the texts on homosexuality literally and not so many other texts. Why do we, for example, read the homosexuality-related texts of the holiness codes literally and as authoritative for today when we ignore almost all of the other parts of those same holiness codes?

It is a challenge to choose one part of our new Confession of Faith to make the test of whether or not someone belongs in the church and ignore other parts of our Confession. For example, if we adhered to every part of the confession equally, all General Conference background Mennonites would need to start washing feet (Article 13 – and clearly proscribed by Jesus, in fact), and no Swiss Mennonites could offer communion to other than baptized adults (Article 12). And we would not be able to officiate or bless any second marriages, especially where there has been a divorce (Article 19). Why do we make some parts of the confession more basic than other parts?

It is a large challenge, I think, to answer the question of what is good news about excluding homosexuals from the church. How is this good news for homosexuals, for the church, and for a skeptical world? I have a particular personal struggle here because I have officiated at funerals of gay people who have committed suicide, ostensibly because they were rejected for their gayness and couldn't bring together being gay and being Christian. They were people who wanted to be in the church.

A corollary to this is the challenge to name what actually is sinful about a covenanted homosexual relationship. What is the sin? How do biblical understandings of sin relate? It seems to me that there are huge challenges facing both the more "open" and the more "closed" position. That alone would indicate that there is considerable dialogue yet necessary. From my point of view, I think that the challenge facing a more closed reading is as big as the one facing a more open reading.

How to Read Scriptures?

How do we read the bible? What tools of study are important to us? What tools and methods have our training, education, and experience made important to us? I mention a few that are important to me. They include:

1) Reading a text very, very carefully. (Reading it in the original languages if possible. I confess to having lost that capability along the way and so have to rely too much on scholars.)

2) Reading in context. What is the larger context of a text: historical, cultural, and thematic?

3) Reading canonically. What are the repeated themes, the big themes, and what are the small themes? How is a text used or referred to in the rest of the canon?

4) Respecting the style of literature used in the text. One reads poetry differently than parables or history, for example.

5) Using as many tools of study as are available to us,

including historical-critical tools, literary tools, and, more recently, "reader/response" tools, along with many others.

6) Read Christologically. Often there is a trajectory or movement forward of themes toward the New Testament (for example, on the question of war and peace). We Mennonites do take the words of Jesus more seriously than other texts.

What I want to say here is that we need to have some consistency in how we read and study and use the Bible from one topic to the next. It is my contention that on the issue of homosexuality, we tend to read the texts differently than we do on other issues. We forget our careful reading. We are inclined to proof text. It is also my contention that I am trying to use the same tools on this issue as I do on every other issue (of course, none of us is ever fully consistent). I am not suddenly abandoning my way of reading the Bible and preaching from the Bible just to come to an open stance on homosexuality. I think I am consistent in my approach.

Examining a Few of the Negative Texts

I do not want to spend much time looking at the texts usually examined when dealing with homosexuality. There are a lot of biblical studies which examine these texts from all sides and do that work much better than I can. I will refer briefly to a few of these texts simply to indicate something of an approach.

In general (and totally over-simplified), it seems to me that whenever sexual acts between same-sex persons are mentioned in the Bible, they are described as "an abomination." Yet the context usually indicates acts, or threats of, violence or rape (Sodom and Gomorrah), or uncleanness as in the Holiness codes of Leviticus (Christians have developed a new set of holiness understandings since Jesus), or male prostitution or exploitive sex (Rom 1). There really is no mention of, and thus no condemnation of, same-sex sexual activity within a permanently committed relationship. This then, is an issue which the Bible does not really address directly.

Genesis 1-3

A number of biblical scholars and theologians, in an effort to be biblical and yet not "proof-texting" in their thinking on homosexuality, begin with Genesis 1-3. They begin with "the ordering of creation," with a natural or creation theology. They acknowledge that the two creation stories and the story of "the fall" do not mention homosexuality at all. But they say that the texts tell us of both the goodness of our bodies and of sex and of the place for and purpose of sex.

One group of these interpreters would say that there is a "maleness" and "femaleness" built into the purpose of creation and that marriage between one man and one woman expresses this ordering. Clearly, a homosexual marriage doesn't. Further, the purpose of sex is, first of all, procreation ("be fruitful and multiply") and secondarily, companionship and pleasure. A homosexual relationship cannot be fruitful in a procreative way. Further, homosexual activity clearly belongs to "the fall," the sinful condition of humans, and is not as God intended in creation.

Another group of interpreters challenges this framework. They would say that if we are basing our opinions on a creation theology, then we have to accept the fact that homosexual orientation was also created by God and thus has to be accepted. They would argue that we shouldn't extrapolate from "maleness and femaleness" in creation to a particular male and particular female. They would say that there are other ways for Christians to be fruitful besides having children. Indeed, can we not give dignity and respect to persons who are single and to persons who choose to be celibate? And, if sexual expression is primarily for procreation, what business do Christian couples have in having sex apart from procreation? Shouldn't couples beyond childbearing years, for example, clearly stop having sex?

As important as biblical work with the creation stories is for finding a reference point to think about homosexuality, I don't think it should be the definitive framework. I don't think it speaks definitively enough, and I don't think a "creation" or "natural theology" is an adequate starting place. I think a "salvation" theology is a better starting place. How is God working to "redeem" a fallen people (that is, all of us, regardless of our orientation). Also more helpful might be a discipleship theology, discerning how followers of Christ can live their lives faithfully.

Genesis 19: Sodom and Gomorrah

What is it that is condemned in this story? Is it homosexuality, or is it violence and rape and lack of hospitality? Here, I use a canonical approach. How does the rest of the Bible use this story?

Deuteronomy 29:20-27, Moses warns his people that their land will be burnt like Sodom and Gomorrah by God's anger if they abandon their covenant with God by serving other gods.

Isaiah 1:9-17; 3:9, The people are likened to Sodom and Gomorrah when they worship with bloody hands and don't seek justice and rescue the oppressed.

Zephaniah 2:8-9, Moab shall become like Sodom and Gomorrah because she has scoffed and boasted against the people of the Lord.

Jeremiah 23:13-14, The people of Jerusalem have become

like Sodom and Gomorrah because they "commit adultery and walk in lies."

Jeremiah 49:17-18, Edom will become an object of horror, like Sodom and Gomorrah, because of the terror she inspires and the pride of her heart.

Jeremiah 50:33-40, God will overthrow the Chaldeans, as God overthrew Sodom and Gomorrah, because she oppressed the people of Israel and Judah.

Ezekiel 16:46-56 (NRSV), The people of Judah have gone a-whoring after other gods. Israel was like Sodom, who had "excess of food, and prosperous ease, but did not aid the poor and needy."

Lamentations 4:6, The punishment of "my people" has been greater than that of Sodom because the precious children of Zion were thirsty, begged for food, and no one gave them anything.

Matthew 10:11-15, Any town that does not accept the disciples of Jesus will, on judgement day, be worse off than the land of Sodom & Gomorrah. (See also Luke 10:10-12)

Matthew 11:20-24, The towns of Chorazin and Bethsaida will fare worse on judgement day than Sodom because they do not "repent," though Jesus does works of power there.

Luke 17:26-30, Everyone who tries to make his life secure – cling to things – will lose it like Sodom did and will be left behind like Lot's wife.

2 Peter 2:4-10, Sodom and Gomorrah are an example to the ungodly, to the licentiousness of the lawless, to those who indulge their flesh in depraved lust, and who despise authority.

Jude 5-7, Sodom and Gomorrah were judged for indulging in sexual immorality and pursuing unnatural lust.

What is the central point of the story of Sodom and Gomorrah as used in the rest of the Bible? Only a few of the references are even to "sexual immorality," let alone homosexuality. One could perhaps read homosexuality into "unnatural lust" in Jude. Most of the references are to injustice and idolatry.

Leviticus 18 and 20

These chapters are part of the "holiness code" (Lev 17-26). Homosexual intercourse is an abomination, a depravity. These are words of shame, of taboo, of uncleanness, but probably not of legal law. The Israelites might have shared these "revulsions" with their neighbours, though they alone put them into a "holiness" code. I would make two points here.

My reading is that the particulars of holiness get redefined later in the Bible, especially by Jesus and by the early church. Jesus says, for example, that it is what comes out of the mouth, not what goes into it, that defiles a person (Matt 15:11). For Peter, a whole lifetime of "taboo" was overcome when he was invited to eat what he "knew" to be unclean. "What God has made clean, you must not call profane" (Acts 10:15, NRSV). Holiness is still as important as ever, but what makes for holiness is redefined – mostly away from the definitions of the holiness code in Leviticus.

If we are going to take as authoritative for us today the naming of same-sex intercourse as "an abomination," then we should at least be consistent in taking everything else in the holiness code as binding for us today too. We have, in fact, not applied literally most things in it. Most of us would not want to live by that code. For example, we clearly see menstruation as natural today, not as unclean.

I am especially interested in one particular part of the holiness code, non-sexual in nature, which we have totally overlooked but which probably has far more serious consequences to far more people than same-sex intercourse. Charging interest. Leviticus is clear that it is forbidden to charge interest. "You shall not lend them your money at interest taken in advance, or provide them food at a profit. I am the Lord your God, who brought you out of the land of Egypt, to give you the land of Canaan, to be your God" (Lev 25:37-38, NRSV).

Psalm 15 is very explicit about how evil charging interest is. Those who may dwell on God's holy hill are those who do not lend money at interest and do not take a bribe against the innocent.

Ezekiel says charging interest is worthy of the death penalty (18:8-17; 22:12). Charging interest is also forbidden in Deut 23:19-20, and Neh 5:6-13. A case could be made that Jesus has similar leanings in the parable of the unforgiving servant (Matt 18:23-35).

It seems to me that the issue of charging interest, in fact, affects millions of people in our world today. In fact, whole nations are impoverished because of the interest debt they owe. Charging interest is a major cause of the impoverishment of many people. It is probably for this reason that the Bible condemns it. (How many people are hurt by a faithful, monogamous, homosexual relationship?) So why do we not read these texts in the same literal way? Why do we choose one way of reading some texts and a different way of reading others? (Of course, we all do this, and need to do this, but here there seem to be particular contradictions in the way we read Leviticus.)

Romans 1:26-27

Romans 1:26-27 is perhaps the most difficult to deal with for those of us who are on the "open" side of this issue. This, after all, comes in the New Testament and comes from Paul. But even here, there is some ambiguity of purpose and thus of interpretation. The Greek words Paul uses here are somewhat ambiguous. Some biblical scholars say that what Paul is condemning here is pederasty, common in both Greece and Rome. It refers to the practice of older men forming sexual relationships with young boys. We would call it child abuse. It is exploitative sex.

The context of Romans 1:18 ff. is judgement on idolatry, on not honouring God as God or giving thanks to him. They "worshiped and served the creature rather than the Creator," (Rom 1:25, NRSV), and because of this idolatry, "God gave them up in the lusts of their hearts to impurity" (Rom 1:24, NRSV). Included in this impurity, this taboo or unclean-ness, were men committing shameless acts with men. Some people suggest that the list Paul makes here is the kind of list Jews had as a stock answer as to what gentiles were like. It may very well be that Paul is here summarizing standard Jewish stereotypes of gentiles. (It is similar to other lists.) It is significant, I think, that in Acts 15 (to be treated later), the three conditions that are imposed on gentile Christians all have to do with things connected to idolatry. Surely sex has become an idol in our day. But I don't think we can pinpoint homosexuality as the focal point of that idolatry.

In the larger context of these chapters in Romans, the listing of abominations in Romans 1 is a prelude to chapter 2, where Paul immediately warns us not to judge others, knowing that we ourselves are just as sinful. This leads to chapter 3, which states that no one is righteous – that each of us becomes righteous only through faith in Christ. At any rate, I do not identify in this passage from Romans 1 any of the committed Christian gays and lesbians that I know. By their faith, they demonstrate that they are not idolatrous. However one reads and interprets these "negative" texts, we have to acknowledge that Christians who read the Bible very seriously come out with very different interpretations. This fact alone should caution us to be respectful of "the other side." This fact alone should encourage ongoing dialogue and study with a genuine openness to new insight.

Potential Theological and Biblical Directions

I have become aware that, despite my "listing to one side" of the dialogue, the arguments that resonate most fully with me are those that say that the definitive biblical and theological work on this issue has not yet been done. Of all the books and articles I have read on the subject, the pieces that have grabbed me most are the ones which state that there is much more work to be done. Says David Schroeder (for me, one of the most influential professors at CMBC), now retired:

> Neither inclusion nor exclusion seems the full answer... One alternative might be to declare that we are not yet ready to give a final answer to the problem of inclusion or exclusion of Christians who have made a same-sex covenant. We would declare this to be something we are working on and agree that people need to search together for what will have saving power for all... This option involves trust that with time we will come to know the leading of the Spirit and are committed to bind ourselves to that which is of the Spirit. We need time to work at a new theology based on the Scriptures and on our understanding of the nature of the gospel.[3]

But then there still need to be places of testing, where Christian communities live with the scrutiny of the Holy Spirit to see whether that Spirit will bless covenanted same-sex relationships. Can some of our Mennonite churches be such a place?

Biblical Starting Places for Me

There are no particular biblical texts that those of us who are more open to homosexuals participating in our churches can point to, saying, "God blesses a homosexual covenanted relationship." We will have to look more broadly at the Scriptures. I offer three potential frameworks which I think could be helpful to us: *Listening to Priests, Prophets, Sages, in the context of Worship and Prayers*

One of the frameworks which I felt was very helpful to us at TUMC in our biblical studies was to recognize and work with the various kinds of literature which are included in the canon of our Scriptures. That is, to let the shape of the canon itself help guide our study. That way, one can do detailed biblical study in the larger frameworks that guide the canon itself. This might be the best way to avoid "proof-texting." The central thesis of this framework comes from Walter Brueggemann in his book *The Creative Word*[4] and has been much expanded by Lydia Harder. I am indebted to her work and will try to summarize central points.

Jeremiah 18:18 (NRSV), "Come, let us make plots against Jeremiah—for instruction shall not perish from the priest, nor counsel from the wise, nor the word from the prophet. Come, let us bring charges against him, and let us not heed any of his words."

The Israelites knew that the Scriptures themselves contained different kinds of writings, which, when combined, gave a full sense of God's interaction with, and intentions for, humans. They knew that the priest, the prophet, and the sage represented three very different kinds of sacred Scripture (i.e., *Torah*-Law, *Neviim*-Prophets and *Ketuvim*-Wisdom writings).

The priest represented "The Tradition," the foundations,

the core stories of faith. This core tradition is placed at the beginning of both the Old and New Testaments. The first five books, the Torah, begin the Old Testament. The four Gospels begin the New Testament. These documents are generally understood as the core identity-forming and community-forming knowledge that must be passed on to the next generation. These books are mostly in the form of stories of God's activity with humans – God's saving activity and covenant-making. They show who God is and become identity-forming for people. They know themselves to be the people of God who have experienced God's marvellous salvation. The prohibitions of same-sex sexual activity come from within those sections of the foundational scriptures, which include "practical recipes" for holy living.

The prophet has a very different function. The prophets challenged individuals and the community toward transformation and towards change. Mostly, they pointed out how the people were misusing, messing up, or disobeying the Tradition. But sometimes, they challenged tradition itself as no longer being adequate (e.g., Isaiah 56 when Isaiah moves beyond the words of Moses in Deuteronomy 23 by saying that both the eunuch and the foreigner could be included in the covenant community based on their faithfulness. Or like Jesus who kept saying, "You have heard that it was said... but I say to you"). Or they discovered a new insight locked in the foundational voice and dared utter it. They launched new visions and new possibilities. Theirs was a disruptive voice, often very unwelcome. The prophet so often shook up the community. Jeremiah's people were very angry at his challenging voice. Most communities resisted the prophet. Jesus confronts the Pharisees and scribes – yes, the supposed keepers of the best of foundational traditions. "Therefore I send you *prophets*, *sages*, and *scribes*, some of whom you will kill and crucify, and some you will flog in your synagogues and pursue from town to town" (Matt 23:34, NRSV).

A significant story for me is that of Hosea and Gomer. Hosea is told by God to marry a prostitute. This is in direct violation of the foundational word of Moses. This marriage will demonstrate in a new way God's love for even a faithless people. In his own life story, Hosea will act out an awesome parable of God's love, a prophetic parable which moves beyond the foundational word.

The sage was the wise person who brought to bear the wisdom of the world. (Proverbs, Song of Solomon, Ecclesiastes, Job, the book of James.) They carried common sense and a broad knowledge. Often, they gave very practical advice. They could bring in knowledge from outside the community (like we can bring in the knowledge of philosophy, psychology, sociology, history, science, etc., into our discussions of homosexuality). All life is under God. All truth comes ultimately from God, no matter through which human source, and can be shared with the community.

Job is placed within Wisdom literature. Of particular note in the story of Job for me is the theological wrestling with the problem of suffering. Job and his friends rely on traditional, foundational theology. But it doesn't answer all the questions anymore. Job dares to ask new questions and look for new theological answers. He doesn't really find fully satisfactory new answers but is content when visited by a theophany of God. The story of Job pushes beyond foundational theology.

Priest, prophet, sage. Each of these has important things to say to us about human sexuality and, albeit indirectly, about homosexuality – foundational, identity-forming stuff, prophetic, challenging stuff, and wise, information stuff. We will need to listen to all three. They mirror the very form or canon of the Scriptures.

There is one further kind of Scripture in our Bible which doesn't fit into the other three. That is worship. It is the Psalms. It is the prayers. It is the direct speech of humans with God. Songs of lament, of pain, of praise. They arise out of the conviction that God is indeed with them, and that God longs for communion with them and they long for communion with God. Worship binds everything together. Worship brings *priest, prophet,* and *sage* under one common human need to commune with God and to be renewed personally and communally.

In worship, we acknowledge our need for God and our own inadequate understandings of the Bible, our lives, and our sexuality. In worship, we become one even as we disagree with each other. In worship, we seek a new word from God. For us as Christians, homosexuality must be discussed in the context of prayer and worship, of earnestly seeking the guidance of the Holy Spirit. I think that looking broadly at the shape of the Bible itself can help free us to look broadly at contemporary issues, expecting all four kinds of writing and experience to guide us in our search for truth.

A Covenant Theology

For me, another very broad biblical starting place for our discussion on homosexuality, which seems to have some promise, though as yet largely untapped in the discussion, is with a "covenant" theology. It seems to me that covenant is written centrally and large over the entire Bible. The climax of the salvation story of bringing the people of Israel out of slavery in Egypt was the making of a covenant between God and God's people at Mount Sinai. This covenant informed the relationship between God and people ever after. The prophets critiqued the people for breaking the covenant and called them to return to it. The New Testament was seen as the New

Covenant, with Jesus fulfilling all the promises of what a covenant relationship with God could be like.

I was particularly struck again by Jeremiah's vision of a "new covenant," one where the laws of God would be written on the people's lives and hearts and where everyone, great and small, would "know" the Lord (Jeremiah 31).

The great condemnation and judgement of the prophets had to do with the people breaking that covenant, breaking that loving, obedient relationship with God.

The analogy, or language, used is that of marriage. The people have been "unfaithful." They have "gone a-whoring" after other gods. And yet God is merciful, will invite "his bride" back into covenant relationship, and will forgive her unfaithfulness and remember her sin no more.

Covenant language is not gender specific. Yes, the analogy is marriage. But both genders, both men and women, are the bride. The big, overriding issue is the people's loving relationship with a loving God. The biggest sin is breaking covenant. It is unfaithfulness. It is adultery with other gods.

God's relationship with humans, God's covenant, is the model for our relationships with each other and with our community. It seems to me that covenant language should be the primary framework and language for human relationships, especially for sexual relationships. The vision is for a permanent, committed, loving, faithful, monogamous relationship, which has to be the same for all Christian people, whatever their orientation. The primary sin, in this framework, would not be the making of the covenant itself (including a same-sex covenant) but unfaithfulness to any covenant made. The call is for a very high sexual standard, a very high accountability, and a very strong naming of sin for breaking a covenant once made.

I am aware of how huge a leap this is from condemning homosexual sin to blessing same-sex covenants. Perhaps we can draw a helpful insight from work with the holiness code of Leviticus. There are three levels or stages of separation between humans and God. Some things are unclean, an abomination, a taboo. When humans are touched by these things, they are unclean. Some things though, can become clean through proper ceremonies or simply through time. A menstruating woman, for example, can move from unclean to clean through time and ceremonies. Being holy, or close to God, can only be done by moving from "clean" to holy, never from "unclean" directly to holy. There is insight in that for our day, too. For people who see homosexuality as unclean, an abomination, and a taboo, it will not be possible to move directly to "holy," to a blessing of a same-sex covenant. There would first have to be a movement from unclean to clean. Perhaps this can happen as we experience and observe healthy, covenanted same-sex relationships. For a younger generation, there is far less of a sense of the unclean or abomination to homosexuality. It is already clean, or at least neutral. (This does not mean necessarily acceptance.) For this generation, the movement from clean to holy – that is blessing – will not feel like a big leap.

I offer this "biblical/theological" direction focused on covenant as one which holds, for me, some promise but which has not been tested or thought through or reflected on adequately in light of our discussion.

The Trajectory of Inclusion

More generally, it seems to me that the movement of the Bible is over and over again in the direction of drawing into the community and into the covenant persons who were on the margins. The story of God's people from Abraham on was to include the "gentiles" in the outpouring blessing of God. Even some people who were specifically excluded by Moses were later included. The Eunuch and the foreigner (excluded by Moses in Deut. 23) are invited in by Isaiah (Ch. 56). Ruth, the Moabite (Moabites are specifically excluded in Deut. 23), is welcomed in. Jesus constantly draws people to himself who were "sinners on the margins." He announces at times that the faith of a foreigner is greater than anything he has seen in all of Israel. And Paul fought the battle to include the gentiles.

I have also found very helpful the discussion around the Jerusalem Conference described in Acts 15. This story follows the stories of Peter's transformation into one who could enter Cornelius's house and see evidence of the Holy Spirit in this gentile's life. Acts 15 is a very useful "model" of how the early church struggled with issues of "inclusion and exclusion" around gentiles. They took the tradition, the Scriptures, seriously but also looked for evidence of the work of the Holy Spirit. This itself was a new paradigm for processing issues. Eventually, the early church accepted Christian gentiles because, clearly, the Holy Spirit was evident in their lives. They released these gentiles from some of the laws clearly stated in the Scriptures but bound them to others.

The people who came to Paul and Barnabas in Antioch, as recorded in Acts 15:1, were on good solid biblical ground in insisting on circumcision for all gentiles coming into the church. Moses had laid down this law, and it had never been challenged, even by Jesus. The debate is lively and hot. Who can be included, and who must be excluded? The Holy Spirit seems to intrude. At least, Peter witnesses the work of the Holy Spirit in the lives of un-circumcised gentiles. James then says that God is doing a new thing. And eventually, the conference declares itself ready to include gentile Christians into their community.

But they will ask these gentiles to keep three aspects of

Jewish law even as they release them from large chunks of the Jewish law. They will be asked to abstain from things polluted by or sacrificed to idols, from sexual immorality, and from whatever has been strangled and from blood.[5] Sylvia stated:

> All these stipulations revolve around the issue of idolatry: what the gentile believers are being asked to put off is precisely those things that are central to a life of idol worship in the Roman empire. Just as in Romans one where idolatry was at the root of the depravity of the gentile life, the root behind the sexual immorality, the slander and gossip, the envy and covetousness, the deceit and unfaithfulness; so the Jerusalem council discerned that idolatry was at the heart of the worship that the gentiles now had to abandon.

James then summed up the discussion and the decision in the letter he wrote to the gentiles in Antioch. "It has seemed good to the Holy Spirit and to us to impose on you no further burden than these essentials" (Acts 15:28, NRSV). And the believers in Antioch received this letter with great joy.

To me, the story of Acts 15 is a very helpful model for all of our discussions of inclusion and exclusion. The Tradition is taken seriously, but so is the evidence of the work of the Holy Spirit. gentiles are included now without requiring circumcision and other dearly held laws. However, restrictions are placed on them regarding practices connected with idolatry.

We might also reflect on the fact that we have, for the most part, abandoned two out of the three of those restrictions because they are no longer connected with idolatry for us. We no longer abstain from things polluted by or sacrificed to idols or from whatever has been strangled and from blood. In other words, our culture has changed, and so these things are no longer connected to idolatry for us. But we do continue to say that sexual morality is still very important to us.

Can we too look for evidence of the Holy Spirit and the blessing of God in the lives of Christian committed same-sex partnerships? Can we release them from laws that bind unnecessarily and bind them only to being committed to following Christ in their relationship? Such a commitment would, in my mind, include challenging them to be faithful to their covenant, abstaining from promiscuity, and living in such a way that no part of their lives, including their sexual lives, would become idolatrous.

Conclusion

I said earlier in this piece that I resonate most with those voices that say the best and final word has not yet been spoken around our understandings of human sexuality and homosexuality. To me, this means we will need to take time, a great deal of time yet, before the church can say with full clarity and assurance that it has a clear message and perspective from God's Holy Spirit. In the meanwhile, we need to make some discernments.

It seems to me that Jesus continually rejected the "stereotyping" by which a group of people were seen in one way. He moved directly to speaking personally with an individual. In other words, his was a pastoral response, not a rule-bound response. It would help us so much if we could be free to make pastoral responses to all people in the church rather than stereotypical or rule-bound responses to "groups" of people. As a group and as a stereotype, I am afraid that "homosexual" has become a symbol for everything that is bad in Western sexuality generally, and they become scapegoats for our own discomfort with, and inability to deal in a healthy way with, our own sexuality.

I have said that I am on the "open" side of this issue and can see the possibility that God will bless a loving, committed, monogamous covenant between two Christians of the same gender. My personal convictions and beliefs lead me to a place where I can affirm "covenant" making between two same-sex persons. I believe they need the support and blessing of the church and need to be held accountable by the church. But I also would acknowledge that I, as a Mennonite pastor, would not feel that I am able to "officiate" such a "blessing" at this time. The office of pastor belongs to the church, not to one personally. I need to respect the choices of the church that holds that office.

While we continue to struggle with the huge issue of understanding biblical and Christian understandings and perspectives on human sexuality, I commend to us all an article by James Reimer in the November 4 issue of the *Canadian Mennonite* entitled, "Tolerance, exclusion....or forbearance?"[6]

> With forbearance, one holds strong commitments and tries
> to convince others to share them, while learning to live with
> those who differ from us.

I believe that our communities of faith should be places where all those who confess that Jesus is Lord and who practice such commitment should be welcomed. I do see the evidence of the work of the Holy Spirit in the lives of some Christians who are homosexual. I think the church should challenge all Christians, heterosexual or homosexual, to be fully Christian in their relationships and in their sexual ethics.

I pray "forbearance" for all of us as we continue to struggle with our differences and as we continue to pray for God's leading.

3. Resolution on Human Sexuality

General Conference Mennonite Church, 1986, Saskatoon[1]

Our Affirmation

We affirm that sexuality is a good and beautiful gift of God, a gift of identity and a way of being in the world as male and female.

We affirm that we can feel positive about our bodies and our sexuality because we know our Creator.

We affirm that sexual drives are a real part of our lives, but that the satisfaction of those drives is not the chief good in life.

We affirm both the goodness of singleness and the goodness of marriage and family in the Lord.

Our Confession

We confess that our sexual attitudes and practices too often fall far short of the biblical standards. No one can boast of perfection in this area.

We confess that sexism lingers among us, damaging the self-esteem of women and hindering their full contribution to personal relationships and to the church, and denying men a true understanding of themselves.

We repent of our wrong view of the body which keeps us from speaking openly and honestly about our bodies, including our sexual nature.

We repent of our judgmental attitudes and our slowness to forgive each other when we fail, a sign of lack of compassion.

We confess our fear and repent of our rejection of those of us with a different sexual orientation and of our lack of compassion for their struggle to find a place in society and in the church.

We repent of our permissiveness which too often leads to premarital and extramarital sexual relationships.

We repent of our failure to maintain healthy and growing marriages.

Our Covenant

We covenant with each other to study the Bible together and expand our insight into the biblical teachings relating to sexuality. We understand the Bible to teach that sexual intercourse is reserved for a man and a woman united in marriage and that violation of this teaching is a sin. It is our understanding that this teaching also precludes premarital, extramarital and homosexual sexual activity. We further understand the Bible to teach the sanctity of the marriage covenant and that any violation of this covenant, including spouse abuse, is sin.

We covenant with each other to mutually bear the burden of remaining in loving dialogue with each other in the body of Christ, recognizing that we are all sinners in need of God's grace and that the Holy Spirit may lead us to further truth and repentance. We covenant compassion and prayer for each other that distrustful, broken, and sinful relationships may experience God's healing.

We covenant with each other to take part in the ongoing search for discernment and for openness to each other. As a part of the nurture of individuals and congregations we will promote congregational study of the complex issues of sexuality, through Bible study and the use of *Human Sexuality in the Christian Life: A Working Document for Study and Dialogue.*

Finally, we covenant with God that as we discern his will for our lives and our fellowship, we will seek to obey it, through his grace and strength.

4. Resources on Abuse Reporting and Prevention

Into Account — "Support for survivors & allies seeking justice, accountability, & recovery in Christian contexts." They are survivor advocates and also offer services to institutions, working with religious contexts but identifying as "non-faith-based." (https://intoaccount.org/)

SAFEZONE: Promoting Healthy Boundaries in Christian Camps, and more generally for churches, ***Sacred Trust: Fostering Safe Space in Congregations.*** Both resources are by Carol Penner and many others are available as free downloads: commonword.ca

Denominational organizations like Mennonite Central Committee also produce excellent resources: https://abuseresponseandprevention.ca/

Faithtrust Institute (Seattle — faithtrustinstitute.org)[1] Online they offer extensive annotated bibliographies on sexual domestic violence and clergy sexual assault resources.[2] One of their resources is a 24-page *Handbook for Advocates* (free pdf available at vawnet.org), on *Faith and Intimate Partner Violence.*

Peace Theology and Violence Against Women: In 1992 a pitoval book was published, a collaboration by Mennonite women theologians and other professionals, aimed at uncovering gender-based violence, especially sexism and patriarchal abuse by men against women: Elizabeth G. Yoder, ed., *Peace Theology and Violence Against Women*, Occasional Papers No. 16 (Elkhart, IN: Institute of Mennonite Studies, 1992).

5. Violence & Abuse - Liturgical Resource

A Worship Service Naming this Reality: February 2, 1997

The following text includes many, but not all elements, which were used in a worship service.[1] It is provided here, in this revised form, as a template for others who may wish to develop a similar service, which would ideally include updated, local and contextual elements and texts. Statistics found below should be updated and modified. Hymn references are from *Hymnal: A Worship Book*, Mennomedia, 1992.

Prelude
   Hymn #640 *This is a Day of New Beginnings*
   Hymn #105 *Christ, We Do All Adore Thee*

Introduction to the theme of this service

As many of you are aware, today's service is dedicated to the theme of violence against women. There are many strands that were woven to create today's service.

One of these strands came from events within our own

community, noting our own struggles in dealing with issues of violence toward some of the women in our congregation. The coordinating team and reference teams that have been working on this issue over the past year agreed with the suggestion that a service focusing on the theme of violence against women would be an important step in our ongoing attempts to understand some of these issues. Yet, if anything must be emphasized, this is but one strand. Just as Tamar ripped her clothes to express her despair after she was raped, violence rips apart the lives of women daily. It is not just something that happens "out there" or an activity that accompanies military repression. It is an ongoing struggle and burden that women carry throughout the world, throughout this city, and within this church.

You will notice that the order of service has designated four primary sections. As the organizing committee discussed what we wanted to emphasize, one point was very clear: it is *our* violence and *our* pain that we wish to experience and understand today. It should be noted that the emphasis on violence against women does not reflect an attempt to dismiss or downplay issues of violence toward men; to minimize one tragedy at the expense of another accomplishes nothing. It was our attempt, however, to emphasize that violence against women has its own story – whether it be the numbers involved, the type of relationship between abuser and victim, or the type of assaults perpetrated; violence against women has its own story. We as a congregation have already known this story, though we may not have acknowledged it as such or may not have been as sensitive to it as we could have been.

So today, we invite you to a journey of songs, prayers, stories, and ceremony. The stories (NB: which are not included here), I should add, have come from a variety of sources: books and studies regarding violence against women in Canada, material from MCC, and stories written by women in our congregation. So again, we invite you into this journey and hope that you continue it and the weaving together of the torn fabric of our lives at a healing service that is being planned for a later date.

Introduction to the music of the service

When planning the music for today's service, I struggled to find hymns with words appropriate for our difficult theme of "violence against women." At first, it seemed that the only sung response possible was a plea for mercy, "Kyrie Elieson" (Lord have mercy), which has been used in Christian litanies from the earliest days of the Eastern church onward. We will respond to times of prayer with the Kyrie throughout the service.

But words of adoration and commitment through the powerful, meaningful hymns of "Christ do all adore thee" and "Obey my Voice" also needed to be sung.

However, the words of new hymns written in the past 15 years or so became compelling in their ability to express different parts of this service, in spite of the relative unfamiliarity of their tunes. Only later did I discover that Brian Arthur Wren, born in 1936, wrote the texts of these three hymns – "When grief is raw," "Woman in the night," and "This is the day of new beginnings." For me, this was a powerful leading of the Holy Spirit. May the Spirit lead us in our worship through words, hymns, and music.

Call to Worship

Silence: Time of private prayer and meditation.

Choral Response: Kyrie (sung by women walking into the meeting place).

Naming our Violence

Psalm 55:1-3, NRSV

Give ear to my prayer, O God; do not hide yourself from my supplication. Attend to me, and answer me; I am troubled in my complaint. I am distraught by the noise of the wicked. For they bring trouble upon me, and in anger they cherish enmity against me.

We name our violence (After each naming we will rip a cloth)

Sexual assault

One in four women in Canada will be sexually assaulted at least once in their lifetime.

Cloth ripped

Physical assault

Between 10% and 20% of Canadian women will be physically assaulted at least once.

Cloth ripped

Child abuse

1 in 3 girls and 1 in 7 boys will be sexually abused by the time they reach 18.

Cloth ripped

Date rape

In a research study involving 304 Toronto high school students, 11% of the young women interviewed reported physical abuse, 17% reported verbal abuse, and 20% reported sexual abuse within a dating relationship.

Cloth ripped

Incest

1 out of 6 women are victims of incest.

Cloth ripped

Wife assault

22% of women in Ontario are physically or sexually assaulted by their partner at some point during their relationship. 14% of married women will be sexually assaulted at least once by their husband.

Cloth ripped

Murder

In Canada, two women are murdered every week by their intimate partner. A woman in Canada is nine times more likely to be murdered by her partner than she is by a stranger.

Cloth ripped

Prayer

As we approach this time of prayer, I would ask that you be very still and not touch anyone whom you may now be touching. Feel the separate-ness, feel the disconnection. Experience this place and this time as if you were totally alone.

God, on this day we have heard upsetting and frightening numbers and facts. Numbers and facts that are not out there but in here, in this meeting room, in our lives. We approach you as people of violence and as people of pain who need you. Meet us in our place and in our pain.

Choral Response: Kyrie

Naming our Pain

My heart is in anguish within me, the terrors of death have fallen upon me. Fear and trembling come upon me, and horror overwhelms me. And I say, 'O that I had wings like a dove! I would fly away and be at rest; truly, I would fly far away; I would lodge in the wilderness; I would hurry to find a shelter for myself from the raging wind and tempest.'

It is not enemies who taunt me—I could bear that; it is not adversaries who deal insolently with me—I could hide from them. But it is you, my equal, my companion, my familiar friend, with whom I kept pleasant company; we walked in the house of God with the throng. Let death come upon them; let them go down to Sheol; for evil is in their homes and in their hearts. Psalm 55:4-8, 12-14 NRSV

Poem by Virginia Lepp

I remember the time of not knowing,
    Not with fondness, but just as fact.
    More clearly, I remember the moment when not knowing was no longer an option.
    Getting acquainted with a work colleague over tea,
    Chatting about family.
    "Do you have any siblings?", I asked.

*"I had a sister who was raped and killed in Montreal
last spring".*
Stated as fact – just like that.
Never again will I not know.
And now, years later, I know more:
A friend raped in her home
Teenage date rape shaping a grown woman's life
A woman and child shot by husband and father
A family fleeing from an alcoholic's rage
And now, years later, I know more;
The fear, no, terror, of threatening words.
So easy to come out of one person's mouth,
As if anyone could kid about that.
I know now;
How to look behind me,
The comfort of a little black alarm,
To scan the crowd for that unwanted familiar face.
I know now;
Not to expect safety;
How hurtful people's light reactions can be;
To take another's fears seriously;
To look out for my needs and to seek safe places.
I remember a time of not knowing,
Not with fondness, but just as fact.

[add stories here from local context]

*For example, On December 6, 1989, 14 women were
murdered at the University of Montreal.*

Hymn #637 *When Grief is Raw* (Verse 1 sung by soloist)
Prayer
As we approach this time of prayer, I ask that you become

aware not only of loneliness but also of pain; of times that perhaps you had wondered 'where was God'? Remember times that you experienced abandonment, despair, and violation. The Psalmist cried out words of despair; 'My God, my God, why have you abandoned me?' The stories we have heard have spoken of many experiences, of boundaries crossed, of boundaries violated – of bruises and broken hearts – of broken trust, fear, anger, terror, abandonment, and grief. These scars from violence run deep into our souls.

Hear our stories, God, and meet us in the place of our deepest pain.

Choral response: Kyrie (#144, sung by the congregation).

Time of private prayer and meditation

Naming our confession

Hymn #637 *When Grief is Raw* (vs. 2 sung by duet)

> But I call upon God, and the Lord will save me. Evening and morning and at noon I utter my complaint and moan, and he will hear my voice. He will redeem me unharmed from the battle that I wage, for many are arrayed against me. God, who is enthroned from of old, will hear, and will humble them—because they do not change, and do not fear God. My companion laid hands on a friend and violated a covenant with me with speech smoother than butter, but with a heart set on war; with words that were softer than oil, but in fact were drawn swords. Psalm 55:16-21, NRSV

Prayer

God, you have heard our acknowledgment and our confession. You know our sins, and you know our scars. May we call upon you, that you will hear our cries and rescue us from our own violence and the violence of others. May we hear the cries of our sisters, may we see their tears, may we feel their pain. And may we offer our hope. Amen.

Choral Response: Kyrie (Sung by congregation)

Ceremony of Commitment

Hymn #223 *Women in the Night*

The words to this hymn were prompted when Wren thought of the women around Jesus. The stanzas name eight places where the lives of women converged with Jesus' life. These glimpses are all from the Gospels, beginning with the mother, Mary. As we sing the hymn, be aware of the familiar stories which are easily recognizable through the few short phrases Wren used to create each vignette. The tune was written by Marilyn Houser Hamm, one of the most gifted and sensitive hymnologists I have had the privilege to sing with. She titled the hymn tune *CANDLE* to reflect the element of struggle that so many feel, particularly women, in their journey for faith and wholeness.

Introduction to our ceremony of commitment

We have named our violence. We have heard stories of our pain. We have made our confession. And now, we want to make our commitment in a ceremony of commitment. We do so by gathering the cloth and by lighting a candle.

I invite you, if you feel so called, to make your commitment by going to the back of the church and picking up a piece of cloth to bring forward and place in the basket. Then, light a candle. At the beginning of this service, as we named our violence, we tore cloth, symbolizing our "torn-ness" and our pain. Now, we want to collect pieces of cloth, which we will at a later time stitch together into a quilt of healing.

Why come forward? Perhaps for a wide spectrum of reasons. Perhaps to acknowledge the violence within us and to commit ourselves never to cause pain to another by it. Perhaps to commit ourselves to do all within our power to make our relationships, our home, and our church a "safe" place for all within these spheres. Perhaps to commit ourselves to speak up when others are being violated, thus becoming advocates for them. Perhaps our commitment, if we have been personally wounded by violence, is to embark upon – or to continue – a healing journey. This requires so much courage.

There may be many reasons to come forward in an act of commitment, surely many more than I have mentioned. In your coming, you will bring a piece of cloth to help create a quilt of healing. In lighting a candle, you will add light to the light of hope. It will be a profound and beautiful thing. Come then if you feel moved to and if you feel called to.

Hymn #223 *Women in the Night* (sung while we come forward with candle and cloth).

Offering

We remind ourselves that part of our offering is passed on to Mennonite Central Committee, which is currently involved in developing programs in Ontario to help those who have experienced violence and those who have perpetrated violence.

Closing hymn #640 *This is a Day of New Beginnings*
Benediction

List of Scripture Passages: Sermons 1-17

Below is an overview of which texts served as the basis for the sermons, which were read before the sermon was delivered. It is recommended to read the passages at the start of the sermon. This is a complete listing of all verses referenced.

1. Psalm 55:12-13; Genesis 1 & 2
2. Ephesians 2:1-10
3. Psalm 55:6-21; Matthew 25: 34-36
4. Philippians 2:1-11
5. Song of Songs
6. 2 Samuel 11:1-5, 12: 1-9
7. Esther
8. Hosea 11
9. Judges 13-16
10. Ruth 1-4, Deuteronomy 24:19-22
11. 1 Corinthians 6:12-20; Gen. 1 & 2; Psalm 139:12-13
12. Genesis 2
13. Matthew 16:13-20; Jeremiah 18:18; Matthew 23:34
14. Genesis 1 & 3; Song of Songs
15. Romans 12:9-10
16. 1 Corinthians 13:4-6
17. Ephesians 3:14-19

Notes

Introduction: An Interview with the Author

1. Lydia Neufeld Harder, *Obedience, Suspicion and the Gospel of Mark: A Mennonite Feminist Approach to Biblical Authority* (Waterloo: Wilfred Laurier Press, 1998).

2. Kissing Frogs – and Other Valentine's Intimacies

1. Wes Seeliger, *Faith at Work Magazine* (February 1972), 13. quoted in Bruce Larson, *Ask Me to Dance* (Waco, TX: Word, 1972), 11-12.

3. Shelter in a Time of Storm – Sexual Abuse

1. "Where is the church when violence strikes home," a sermon preached February 28, 1988, at College Mennonite Church, Goshen, Indiana.
2. Statistics taken from late 1980s and for updates (Canada and USA) see: https://canadianwomen.org/ and https://ncadv.org/STATISTICS

4. In the Image of God

1. Rosemary Radford Ruether, *Sexism and God Talk* (Boston: Beacon Press, 1983), 61.
2. See Sandra M. Schneiders, *Women and the Word: The Gender of God in the New Testament and the Spirituality of Women* (Paulist Press, 1986).
3. Many people have speculated about whether Jesus had a sexual relationship with Mary Magdalene or whether he was in fact married. They suggest that later interpreters excluded that fact.

5. A Symphony of Sensuality

1. Translated from the original, written c.1136.

9. Sex, Intimacy & Violence – the Story of Samson

1. Anne Morrow Lindbergh, *Gift of the Sea* (New York: Pantheon, 2005), 96.

11. A Biblical Perspective on Human Sexuality

1. David Augsburger, *Be All You Can Be* (Carol Stream, IL: Creation House, 1970), 69.
2. Carolyn Holderread Heggen, *Women's Concerns* magazine, March-April 1992, 3.
3. Cited in Carolyn Holderread Heggen, *Sexual Abuse in Christian Homes and Churches* (Eugene: Wipf & Stock, 2006), 61.

13. Accountability, Priests, Prophets and Sages

1. David Schroeder, 'Homosexuality: Biblical, Theological, and Polity Issues' in Norman Kraus, ed., *To Continue the Dialogue* (Kitchener: Pandora, 2001) 75.
2. David Schroeder, "Discerning What Is Bound in Heaven," in A.J. Dueck, ed., *The Bible and the Church* (Winnipeg, MB: Kindred Press, 1988), 63-74.
3. The *Believers Church Commentary,* on the Gospel According to Matthew insists that it is on Peter the rock that Jesus will build the church. Richard B. Gardner, *Matthew: Believers Church Bible Commentary* (Scottdale: Herald Press, 1991).
4. I am indebted to my wife Lydia's reflections on these concepts as she has published in Lydia Neufeld Harder, *The Challenge is in the Naming* (Winnipeg: CMU Press, 2018), 311f.

IV. Weddings and Marriage

1. *Celebrating Christian Marriage*, Worship Series, No. 6. (Newton, KS: Faith and Life Press, 1980).

14. Sexuality in the Wedding

1. Revision of article published in *Vision: A Journal for Church and Theology*, Fall 2008, 33-40. Also published in Lydia Neufeld Harder, *The Challenge is in the Naming: A Theological Journey* (Winnipeg: CMU Press, 2018), 297-305.
2. William Willimon, *Worship as Pastoral Care* (Nashville: Abingdon Press, 1979), 127.

16. An Encompassing Intimacy

1. Kahlil Gibran, *The Prophet* (New York: Knofp, 1923).

2. An Essay on Homosexuality

1. Michael King, *Fractured Dance: Gadamer and a Mennonite Conflict over Homosexuality* (Telford: Cascadia, 2001), 62.
2. Hubert Schwartzentruber, *Jesus in Back Alleys: The Story and Reflections of a Contemporary Prophet* (Telford: Cascadia, 2002) 112.
3. David Schroeder, 'Homosexuality: Biblical, Theological, and Polity Issues,' 72.
4. *The Creative Word: Canon as a Model for Biblical Education* (Minneapolis: Fortress Press, 1982).
5. I am indebted here to a sermon preached in TUMC by Sylvia C. Keesmaat in the fall of 2002. Sylvia is a professor of New Testament at Toronto School of Theology.
6. Reprinted in A. James Reimer, *The Dogmatic Imagination: The Dynamics of Christian Belief* (Waterloo: Herald Press, 2003), 88.

3. Resolution on Human Sexuality

1. *Saskatoon '86: General Conference Mennonite Church forty-fourth triennial sessions ... minutes* (Newton: General Conference Mennonite Church, 1986), 10.

4. Resources on Abuse Reporting and Prevention

1. Previously Alban Institute provided resources and some of its projects were continued by the Center for Congregations in Indianapolis but the Interfaith Sexual Trauma Institute (Saint John's Abbey) is no longer active.
2. https://www.faithtrustinstitute.org/resources-documents/ SexualDomesticViolenceBiblio.pdf
    https://www.faithtrustinstitute.org/news/update-to-clergy-sexual-assault-bibliography

5. Violence & Abuse - Liturgical Resource

1. The original text for this service included many more details, including the names of the participants who led the service, as well as other stories and a second poem, which we did not choose to reprint here.

Acknowledgments

I wish to express deep gratitude to all those who have trusted me with their stories and spurred my ongoing exploration of themes related to sexuality in the Bible. My clinical training in London, Ontario played a huge role in helping me connect with and understand my emotional make-up, which significantly impacted my pastoral ministry and my marriage. I credit that year with starting a major shift in my personal life, marriage, and ministry.

At TUMC I was blessed by working together with a preaching team: of four members, chosen by the congregation, who challenged me, inspired me, planned the preaching ministry with me, and preached about half of all Sundays. They encouraged me to preach about human sexuality.

At TUMC, a committee developed the original version of "Appendix 5, Violence & Abuse - Liturgical Resource" and I am especially grateful to Virginia Lepp for her permission to reprint her poem here.

I am grateful for permission to reprint reflections used at weddings and previously published materials, which appear here, including; permission to reprint "Sexuality in the Wedding" from *Vision,* a publication of the Institute of Mennonite Studies at Anabaptist Mennonite Biblical Seminary; permission to reprint the "Resolution on Human Sexuality, Saskatoon 1986" granted by Mennonite Church Canada;

permission to reprint letters to the editor in the *Mennonite Reporter* granted by *Canadian Mennonite* magazine.

I am grateful to Gelassenheit Publications — for risking publication "on the edge" — especially to Jonathan Seiling and Janien Reesor, for their support and collaboration on editing, design and production, and to Jeanette Seiling for proofreading, and to Cynthia di Simone for the inspired cover image.

About the Author

Gary Harder grew up on an irrigation farm in Rosemary, Alberta, a unique town with a Buddhist temple, Mormon Temple, and Mennonite Church. Each of these communities had a history of persecution, which created occasions for cooperation and appreciation of each other's heritages.

Gary holds degrees from Canadian Mennonite Bible College (CMBC), Goshen College, Associated Mennonite Biblical Seminaries, and St. Stephen College in Edmonton (DMin). He has served as pastor at Waters Mennonite Church in Lively, Ontario; Yellow Creek Mennonite Church, Elkhart, Indiana; First Mennonite Church, Edmonton, Alberta; and Toronto United Mennonite Church. Gary has served on numerous boards including CMBC, the Leadership Commission of the Conference of Mennonites in Canada, and local ecumenical ministerials.

Gary has published two books, *Dancing Through Thistles in Bare Feet* (Herald Press, 2008) and *The Pastor-Congregation Duet* (Friesen Press, 2018).

Lydia Neufeld Harder grew up on a fruit farm in Niagara. After a stint of elementary school teaching, she attended CMBC and then went on to several years of homemaking and volunteer work in church and community before entering the academic world, graduating from Newman College (MTh) and Toronto School of Theology (TST) (ThD). She directed the Toronto Mennonite Theological Centre (1994-1999) and taught as an adjunct faculty member at TST and Conrad Grebel University College (CGUC).

Lydia has published two books, *Obedience, Suspicion and the Gospel of Mark* (Wilfred Laurier Press, 1998) and *The Challenge is in the Naming* (CMU Press, 2018).

Gary and Lydia's partnership has been important to them from the time they studied Greek together in College and discovered that they had many common interests and commitments to church and ministry. They were married in 1964. Besides co-parenting their three children, they have had opportunities to teach together in Asuncion, Paraguay, and also at CMBC, AMBS, and CGUC. They also spent six months in Cairo with MCC. A particular highlight in their retirement was serving as intentional interim co-pastors in three congregations.

Gary and Lydia live in Luther Village in Waterloo, Ontario. They delight in their three children, nine grandchildren, and two great-grandchildren.